METROPOETICA

Ingmāra Balode
Julia Fiedorczuk
Sanna Karlström
Ana Pepelnik
Zoë Skoulding
Sigurbjörg Þrastardóttir
Elżbieta Wójcik-Leese

with
Katerina Iliopoulou
Alexandra Büchler
Karol Pęcherz
Alan Holmes

Seren is the book imprint of
Poetry Wales Press Ltd.
57 Nolton Street, Bridgend, Wales, CF31 3AE
01656 663018
www.serenbooks.com
Facebook: facebook.com/SerenBooks
Twitter: @SerenBooks

The right of Ingmāra Balode, Julia Fiedorczuk, Sanna Karlstrom, Ana Pepelnik, Zoë Skoulding, Sigurbjörg Þrastardóttir and Elżbieta Wójcik-Leese to be identified as the authors of this work has been asserted in accordance with the Copyright, Designs and Patents Act, 1988.

Copyright © Metropoetica 2013

ISBN 978-1-78172-128-5

A CIP record for this title is available from the British Library.

The publisher acknowledges the financial assistance of the Welsh Books Council.

Design by Alan Holmes
Printed in Padstow, Cornwall by TJ International

Metropoetica is a Literature Across Frontiers project:
www.lit-across-frontiers.org
Mercator Institute for Media, Languages and Culture
Department of Theatre, Film and Television Studies
Aberystwyth University, Aberystwyth, SY23 1NN, Wales

www.metropoetica.org

Virtual walks
January – March 2009

Kraków
March 23rd – 27th 2009

Ljubljana
August 30th – September 6th 2009

Riga
September 13th – 16th 2010

Wrocław
April 4th – 10th 2011

Athens
May 1st – 9th 2011

Zoë Skoulding

Metropoetica: Women Writing Cities

The metaphor of the city has often been used to describe the collective, constructed and constantly-changing nature of language. Poetry of the city, meanwhile, locates language within a particular physical context in which the walk and the poem interlock as different means of producing and inhabiting urban space. The intersection between embodied and virtual experience, which increasingly defines the contemporary city, adds another element to this relationship. Metropoetica is a collaborative project devoted to practices of writing and translation that might respond to these conditions. It began in 2009 with a group of seven women poets and translators from different European cities walking, writing and translating, partly online and partly through workshops in Kraków and Ljubljana, with later meetings and performances at poetry festivals in Riga, Wrocław and Athens. Its focus on women writers from a range of European cities has been a means of looking beyond the more traditional poetic frames of the metropolitan and masculine *flâneur*. The writers involved from the start were Ingmāra Balode (Latvia), Julia Fiedorczuk (Poland), Sanna Karlström (Finland), Ana Pepelnik (Slovenia), Sigurbjörg Prastardottir (Iceland), Elżbieta Wójcik-Leese (Poland) and myself (Wales). Others joined the project along the way, and its development was made possible by Alexandra Büchler of Literature Across Frontiers, an organization supported by the European Union Culture Programme that specializes in workshops in which co-translation, often with English as a bridge language, enables the translation of literature between less widely-used languages.

Each of the participating poets inhabits a city, some larger, some smaller, and each of us has been engaged in thinking about where we live as well as the cities in which we have worked collectively. In writing and translating together we have attempted to blur the boundaries between individual and collective experiences of urban spaces, and to explore different possibilities of the poem as a mode of living between and alongside different languages. The language of this book is predominantly English because it is the one we share, and for practical reasons it was necessary to choose one to represent the project in print.

However, there has been extensive translation into other languages for the performances that have taken place during the project, which have been in Polish, Slovenian, Latvian and Greek. Linking embodied experience of the city with the process of writing, we have used film and sound to present our work, aspects of which can be found at www.metropoetica.org. Some of the photographs in this book are records of those performances, which have taken place in the streets, bookshops, bars and arts centres of the places where we have worked together.

The book follows a roughly chronological trajectory, beginning with explorations of our own cities before we had met as a group. Our first collaborative experiment was to explore the city of one of the other poets via an online map, and to send her directions for a walk through her own locality on a route that she may not have chosen herself. We were each able, in this way, to be simultaneously at home and strangers in places we knew well. These virtual walks, made real by someone else, introduced an idea that would develop as the project went on, as we attempted to find ways of defamiliarizing our responses to the cities we visited. In Kraków we walked together through the icy streets, using a pack of cards to decide where to turn, and when to stop and write. In Ljubljana, we focused on the rhythms of the city and ways in which meaning did or didn't run through the shared rhythms of our different languages. In Riga we watched the city watching us through its closed windows, and in Wrocław we sat outside in armchairs, inviting passers-by to read poems with us in a room that had lost its walls and become part of the street. Athens presented us not only with Plato's utopian exclusion of women and poets, but also with the harsh reality of economic collapse, and with North African migrants whose stories remained opaque. Unable to contribute anything but questions to the narratives of a city in such desperate times, we walked and read the graffiti that our Greek friends translated for us. Sanna Karlström's photographs parallel poetry's acts of attention to the small details that constitute the fabric of the city, a visual translation of language's juxtapositions. This book is a selection of texts that follow pixels, strangers, footsteps, birds, philosophers, colours, gestures, children, financial meltdown, words, etymologies and weather across cities and languages.

Explore a city you don't know using an online map.

Choose a route for a walk.

Send it to a poet who lives there.

She follows your directions and writes a poem.

I am guessing which side of the road your house is on, but I think you might be facing south-east. If that's the case, turn left, and left again at the end of your road, which should bring you on to ULICA HERMANA POTOCNIKA. Follow it until you come across JARSKA CESTA, where you turn left. It looks as though there's a way into the cemetery, or maybe this is a park?

You should be able to come up to FFORDD Y COLEG – your starting point – Welsh now. Turn right into what my map calls COLLEGE ROAD again. turn left on to MEIRION ROAD and right into PEACOCK WALK.

When I was looking at the actual map there are a lot of streets without a name

Follow the path that connects nameless, probably dead-end streets. Turn right and take a few steps up to the crossing with and all areas confused about a name

Assuming that you come out of the building so that you have your back to the sea, turn right on to JUHANNUSRUUSUNKUJA, and right again on to SOLSVIKES ALLE, then right twice more on to AURINKORANTA.

turn left and keep walking, crossing TRIJĀDIBAS so that you have your back to the right again on to the edge of the Find your way to the left – westbound? – keeping on whichever because

From FROSTAFOLD to FJORGYN. Walk SASI IELA, turn left and keep walking. appears to be sand. Find your way to the GAFOLD, then HVERAFOLD towards the water, then turn left DARHOFDI road across the park between the water and LO- is on walking the left end walk by the water to STORHOFDI. Turn on to VI-

When in STARAJA RI IELA and continuing water. Now, follow the side of the trees you prefer name HALSABRAUT?).

Does this pond have a name? You want to give it one?

Google Earth refused to show your location. I wrote these directions using a clumsy map I found on the internet. I hope you will get somewhere.

Sigurbjörg Þrastardóttir

Google Earth refused to show your location

Google Earth refused to show my location.
Google Earth is very clever.
Even I don't know where I am.
You need to keep quiet. You need to have secrets.
You need to keep wondering where to go next.

(note: image not from Google Earth for copyright considerations)

9

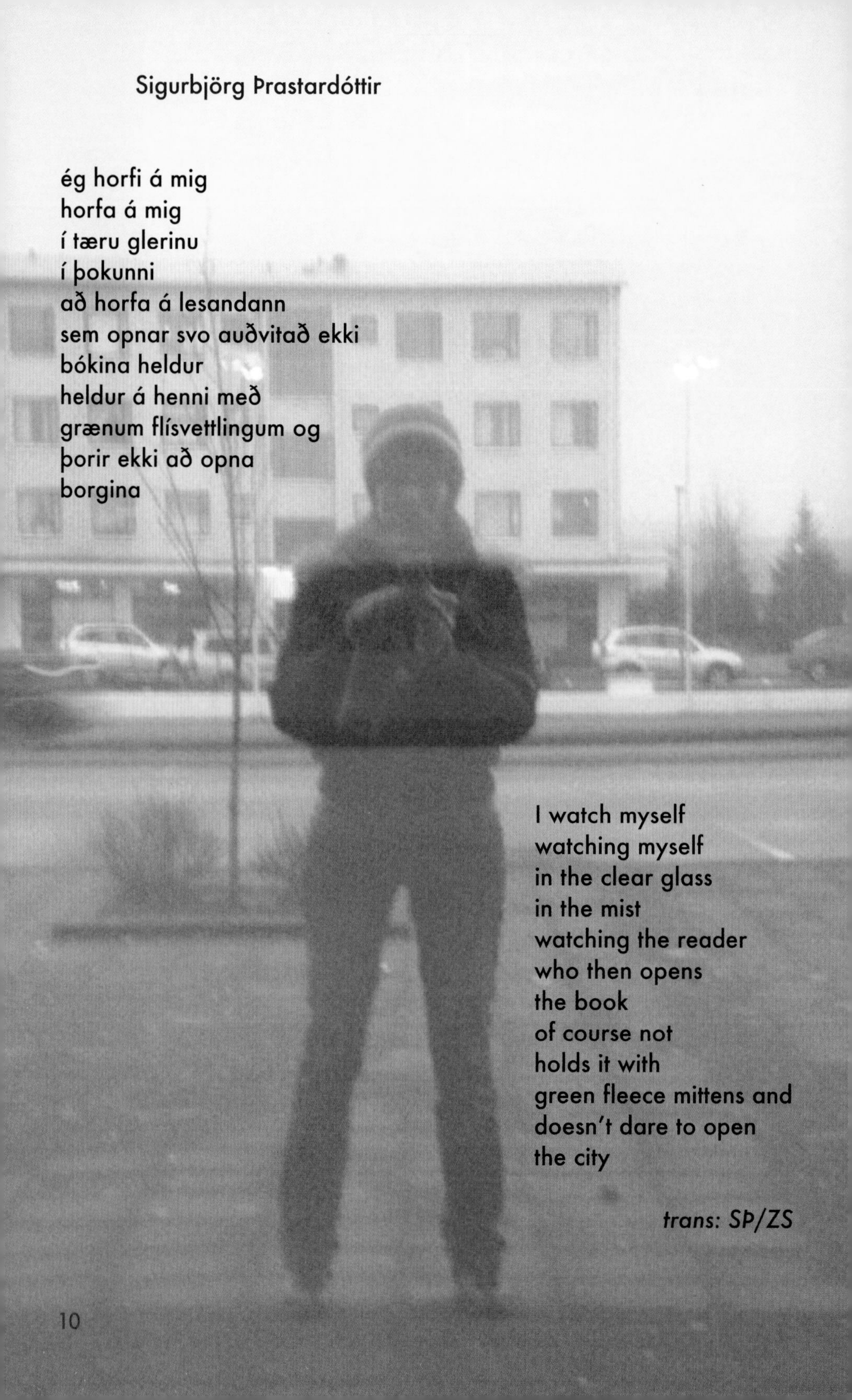

Sigurbjörg Þrastardóttir

ég horfi á mig
horfa á mig
í tæru glerinu
í þokunni
að horfa á lesandann
sem opnar svo auðvitað ekki
bókina heldur
heldur á henni með
grænum flísvettlingum og
þorir ekki að opna
borgina

I watch myself
watching myself
in the clear glass
in the mist
watching the reader
who then opens
the book
of course not
holds it with
green fleece mittens and
doesn't dare to open
the city

trans: SP/ZS

Sanna Karlström

Denying a poem

It was a bad day. Only the weather was good: the air was clear and cold, there was lots of new snow. I was stressed and angry. I was trying to find a flat to rent and everything seemed to go wrong. I had written my directions on a piece of paper, but I was not so sure if I could read my handwriting. I am very good at getting lost, especially in Vuosaari, where I was staying at the time, and where all the houses look the same to me.

I took the walk with Eino, who is also a poet. We were joking about this poetic walk, because I was so tense, swearing all the time, and far from being responsive. First we went to the sea, and of course the sea was beautiful, as always, but especially on this day, one of the first in February when there was real sunlight.

At almost every step we ran into something 'poetic'. When a swan slowly swam to me, and stared for a while right into my eyes, I said I'd rather kick the swan than write about it. But I did not kick the swan. I rented a flat and put the swan in my poem.

Sanna Karlström

Muutto

Lumen maalaama kalustamaton ranta
olen seisonut tikkailla kuin pyrkiäkseni ylös
jaloistaan kömpelö joutsen
asettuu vatsalleen maisemaan
osoittaakseen että ranta on muuten tyhjä

Esine kerrallaan laitettu pois ettei menisi rikki
paperiin kääritty suru ei ole juurikaan tarpeellista
meren tehtävä on huuhdella, minun irrottaa kattolamppu
ja kannatella valoa ettei sitten ole pimeä

Kun naksauttaa silmät auki unia näkemättä
tajuaa olevansa hiekasta tehty ja aurinko nousee
hitaasti talon julkisivua pitkin huoneeseen
jossa seison käsi katkaisimella.

Sanna Karlström

Migration

Unfurnished beach painted by snow
I'm standing half-way up a ladder
a swan clumsy on its feet
settles itself on its belly into the view
to show that the beach is otherwise empty

Things have been put away one at a time so as not to be broken
sorrow wrapped in paper is not worth keeping
the sea's job is to rinse, mine is to get the lamp off the ceiling
and support the lightbulb so it won't be dark

When I click my eyes open without seeing any dreams
understand that I am made of sand and the sun rises
slowly up the façade and into the room
where I stand with my hand on the switch

trans: SK/ZS

Ana Pepelnik

shakes

No wind. Just episodic shakes
of air released by a robin.
Right beside me. We left behind a whole week
of walking between blocks of flats.

Up and down the street several times a day.
People still have their own gardens.
They take good care of them if they're not too busy.
Vegetable plots full of spinach

that nobody cooks.

trans: AP/ZS

Ingmāra Balode

Victory

A virtual walk
becomes more virtual as I turn
backwards and see
snow
changing my screen into a nameless street
on someone's unsigned postcard,
a few grey men falling
under a concrete flag.
The Victory Monument –
but which victory, exactly?
Old men gather here on the 9th of May
to invent their victory.
Tulips travel through the gardens.
Young men, meanwhile,
talk about other victories
rising over the sleepy park
on the grayscale hours marked
slightly pink
by dawn.
Yachts snore on the waterside nearby,
taking part in the victory,
and children take their part
and the elderly take the sun
under the linden trees.

I'm walking in the snow,
rushing towards the word
I must conquer
in this battle with
the calendar. March.

trans: IB/ZS

Julia Fiedorczuk

Brâncuși w Królikarni

Nie da się opowiedzieć co mnie tu przywiodło.
Wiersz byłby dłuższy niż to piękne życie.
A ono jest jak światło przecedzone przez sito drzew.
Oczywiście, teraz. W lipcowej Warszawie, którą chłonę ciałem
bezbolesnym od głowy do stóp.

Teraz? Nie mam innego niż ten kadr z balkonem.
Gruba pani odstawia filiżankę, żeby popatrzeć
na chmury, z których potem spadnie krótki, gęsty deszcz.
Kadr opustoszeje, a przekorny wiatr

przyniesie okruchy rozmowy: klacz, jak się dowiem,
miała na imię Larina. „Żyła jeszcze na pewno
w trzydziestym dziewiątym". To przed Królikarnią.
Starość tych dwojga jest dziwna jak rzeźba.
Czas przed narodzinami, którego nie było.

Czas, „niekończąca się kolumna",
pcha mnie na ulicę już gęstą od słońca.
Wszystko szybko znika, oprócz tych dwóch zdań:
„Lubię koło, ponieważ się toczy.
I lubię kwadrat, bo zostaje w miejscu".

Julia Fiedorczuk

Brâncuși in Królikarnia

I couldn't tell you what has brought me here.
The poem would be longer than this beautiful life.
The life like this light sieved through the trees.
Naturally, right now. In July, in the Warsaw I absorb
with my body painless from top to toe.

Right now? This is my only frame, the one with the balcony.
The fat woman is putting her cup down to glance
at the clouds, which will soon release rain, brief but thick.
The frame will then turn empty, and the mischievous wind

will fetch me snatches of conversation: the mare, I learn,
was called Larina. 'She was most certainly
alive in thirty-nine.' That's before Królikarnia.
The old age of these two peculiar as the sculpture.
Time before my birth, time that didn't exist.

Time, 'this never-ending column,'
prods me onto the street thick with sunshine.
Everything fades fast, except these two sentences:
'I like the circle, because it rolls.
But I like the square, because it stands still.'

trans: EW-L

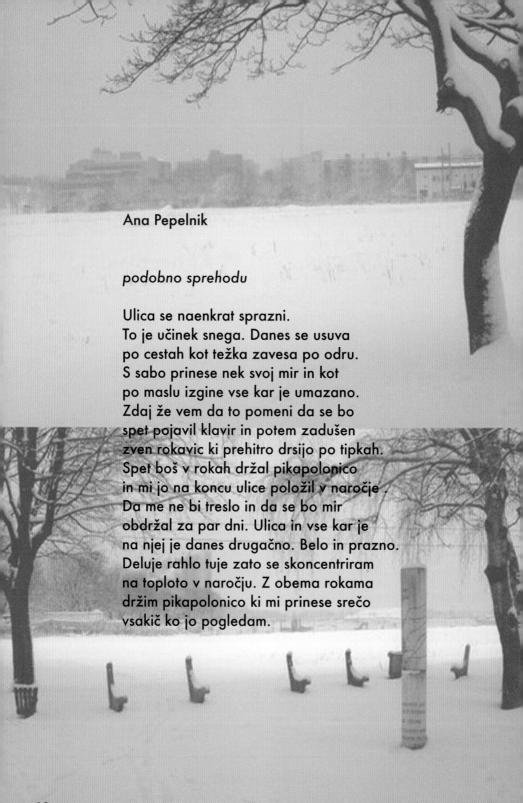

Ana Pepelnik

podobno sprehodu

Ulica se naenkrat sprazni.
To je učinek snega. Danes se usuva
po cestah kot težka zavesa po odru.
S sabo prinese nek svoj mir in kot
po maslu izgine vse kar je umazano.
Zdaj že vem da to pomeni da se bo
spet pojavil klavir in potem zadušen
zven rokavic ki prehitro drsijo po tipkah.
Spet boš v rokah držal pikapolonico
in mi jo na koncu ulice položil v naročje .
Da me ne bi treslo in da se bo mir
obdržal za par dni. Ulica in vse kar je
na njej je danes drugačno. Belo in prazno.
Deluje rahlo tuje zato se skoncentriram
na toploto v naročju. Z obema rokama
držim pikapolonico ki mi prinese srečo
vsakič ko jo pogledam.

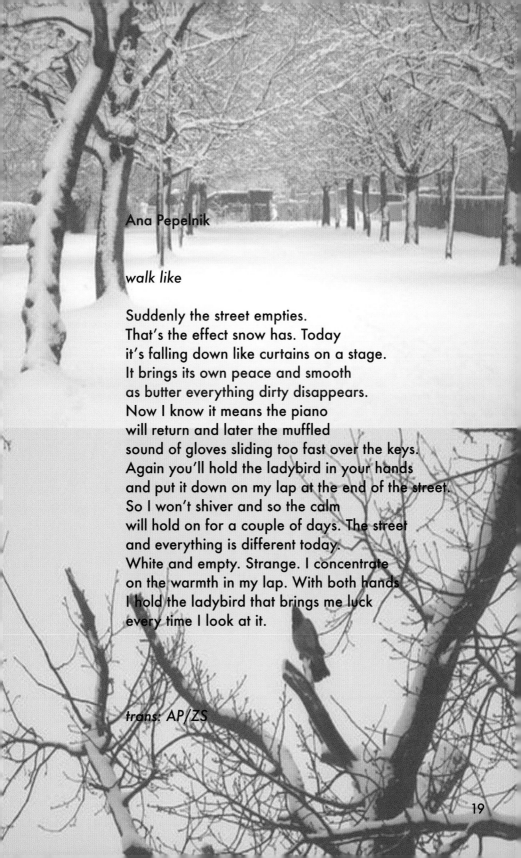

Ana Pepelnik

walk like

Suddenly the street empties.
That's the effect snow has. Today
it's falling down like curtains on a stage.
It brings its own peace and smooth
as butter everything dirty disappears.
Now I know it means the piano
will return and later the muffled
sound of gloves sliding too fast over the keys.
Again you'll hold the ladybird in your hands
and put it down on my lap at the end of the street.
So I won't shiver and so the calm
will hold on for a couple of days. The street
and everything is different today.
White and empty. Strange. I concentrate
on the warmth in my lap. With both hands
I hold the ladybird that brings me luck
every time I look at it.

trans: AP/ZS

KRAKÓW

Ana Pepelnik

Every town contains gaps.

The poem grows out of signs.

It comes out of the night.

The poem is breezing in from the sea.

It drives out of an alley.

When the gap is filled, you can walk further.

You can read further.

Ana Pepelnik / Zoë Skoulding

Mind the Gap

Outside! Birds are
faster than wind.
Sound of wheels
and high heels.
The day is green.

A bee resting on a
baby carriage.
Orange belly of a
robin reflected
on a tree.
Someone's lost an
orange on the path.

Sky spits snow on
hyacinths. Rynek
Główny turns on its
axis under
everyone's feet. A
cigarette stub
glows orange.

včeraj nič novega,
today a morning
glory looks like a
flower

Heads lift to the
sun as the square
spins into shade.
Chatter in all
dimensions over
the crowd's bass
hum.

Rain remains.
Longsounding
drops falling on a
tin gutter in a day
so grey and thin
and brief.

The water seeping
into the stitched
leather of my boots is
evidence that I have
walked through
this poem.

Yesterday's bird
lost in the sunlight
of our garden. My
town is so calm, an
earthquake in
Rome.

Blossom shakes
over cracked soil
 the cry of finches
in a feather's
breadth a breath
where only

leaf tremors hang
in yesterday's
air there was a
handful of dust
look I will show
you.

They were talking
about June in the
middle of April, a
cuckoo in a nest,
some coins in her
pocket. I had a
thought that
wasn't music.

This poem was written in English as a sequence of text messages
between Ana Pepelnik in Ljubljana and Zoë Skoulding in Kraków.

Sanna Karlström

Kraków

Puisto käveli pois
tein siitä muistiinpanoja
kuin joku muu olisi hyräillyt kappaletta
joka on tuttu mutta katkeaa kesken.

Nuo nostivat käsiinsä laudan kuin kadunpätkän.
Nuo olivat harmaita sisältä ja ulkoa.
Satoi ylhäältä, sydämeni oli liuennut takkini sisään.

Koruja myyvä nainen ajatteli jotakin loiston keskellä.

Kraków

The park walked away
I made notes on it
as if someone had been humming a familiar tune
and broken off.

They picked up a plank as if lifting a piece of the street.
They were grey inside and out.
It was raining, my heart had dissolved inside my coat.

A woman selling trinkets had a thought, surrounded by shine.

trans: ZS/SK

Sanna Karlström

Getting There

When I look at maps of cities I know very well, I find it hard to look at the map as it is. I start to see through the drawing to houses, trees, people walking on the pavement, crossing the street. I can imagine myself there, trying to find my keys in my handbag.

When reading a poem, I sometimes get the same feeling, as if I'm looking at a photograph, through it, to the place it was taken. Words and surfaces disappear. The same thing happens when we read something written in a foreign language: the more we learn the language, the more transparent it seems for a while. But then, suddenly, words don't have just one meaning, they won't stay still: there is life in them. We start to see that even what is natural to us in our mother tongue is constantly on the move.

We do not or cannot represent things as they 'really are'. My obsession with detail in poetry must be tied up with this feeling of constant movement, the fluttering of the words and their meanings. I try to get something right, just a tiny detail, and I am hoping that everything else in the poem will find a place around it. I do not collect thoughts, I try to collect details, mistakes and flaws. When we spot a mistake in a photograph, something that seems as though it shouldn't be there, we tend to think it is a proof that the image is genuine. But even when I am trying to get hold of the tiniest detail, it always slips through my fingers and words.

Maps usually try to represent the parts of the city which are relatively simple and unchanging, but we will find our way to our destinations through all the details that the city is full of. We do have perfectly straight and ordered streets in real life (we tend to call them 'unnatural'), but they are almost never without a distraction, even if it's only the birds' unplanned flying.

Things can only be represented because there is someone who observes them, so whatever we are trying to describe, we are describing the process of someone seeing, feeling and thinking. A poem is not still, and there will never be a time when everything has been said. The act of saying, of putting something into words, is a part of this moving and expanding that changes everything. Maps themselves do not get us anywhere. What does is the life we are part of when we step through the map into the city.

Ana Pepelnik / Zoë Skoulding

Tramline (homophonics)

tramvaj je prerasel ulico
čeprav je bilo sonce tisto
ki je bilo tako svetlo
da v dežju nisi videl kosa
še bolj črnega pod mavrico

tramways in grey drizzle hollow lines
cheepings billow in the sonic tissue
below the sweet low dawn
déjà vu nestles in video cues
she bills herself as negative maverick

tramways peel back ululations
where proof lies below sound fissures
a key takes you below the street
of days and days in virtual code
shibboleths pooled in her mouth

Sigurbjörg Þrastardóttir

The Map of Massolit

Metropoetica's working base in Kraków was Massolit, a labyrinthine English-language bookshop that offers customers a hand-drawn map to find their way around.

It's like a treasure map. (The treasure could be a masterpiece, a person, a cup of coffee.) It's handmade, yellowish, as if centuries old. It can't be that old, yet it is a map unlike other maps. It's a 'you are here' in the readable world of civilization. And all map rules are broken. East and west don't work, the Jews are to the east, Asia northbound, Religion is only in the south and New Arrivals are outside the sphere, according to a hand-drawn arrow. The hierarchy of mainstream and marginal is turned inside out; the dominant concepts in the middle, the very first ones to catch the eye are Gay & Lesbian and Women's Studies. Indeed, Old White Western Men do not own a centre here.

Poetry is marked with a swaying arrow that turns everything, as it were, upside down, or inside out; it is an arrow with a swing. It is in the nature of arrows to point straight ahead, or straight to one side; they mark one way, they can't mark a whim, unless they are u-turns (south becomes north becomes south again). Normally, though, signs are put up to ban u-turns, not encourage them. Arrows with a random bend are, then, rare – unless they're handmade, unless they're poetry. And how fitting, say the literary critics, for doesn't poetry just do that, swirl your thoughts around, make a bend in conventional meaning, have you lose your way? Poetry is a whimsical arrow. Economics, on the other hand, has a straight arrow on this map – fittingly arranged, some would say – in the bottom corner, pointing to some obscure future out of the frame.

It is a map of utopian cohabitation. You have the Russians, the Germans, the French and the Spanish piled on top of one other, lying next to each other, lurking behind each other, cultures and religions, neighbours or rivals... depending on how you read a map.

How do you, for that matter, read a map of a bookshop you have never been to? How do you even know it's a bookshop? The best you could do is to pretend you don't know. On the map itself the word 'book' is almost nowhere to be found, so you can fill the gap with whatever you like. Jewish Studies could be studies made by Jews of car speed mechanisms. Psychology could point to therapy rooms: go get your psyche fixed, please. Women's Studies could actually be a row of furnished studies, owned and inhabited by professional women in all fields. Rooms of their own. Photography could be the box where you have your passport photo taken.

There is no non-smoking sign on this map. If you'd never been here you wouldn't know it's a flammable place, made up of old trees turned into books. You wouldn't know it's an ancient forest, a textual world of print, covers, paper moons. Only in the word 'cookbooks' does the word 'book' come up, but by then you're already so swept up by imagination that you're only thinking of food and wine. (The only other use of the word 'books' is guidebooks, ironically, if you still feel you've been misguided.) The adventure map of the Massolit forest has flowers interwoven in it, the plan is swaying, the outlines don't resemble a building at all.

Yet, if you've been here, it makes perfect sense. It even makes more sense than the place itself, as is often the case with maps. You realize that there are in fact no walls and no borders, no boxes of categories. On the contrary, although the real place has shelves that might seem like limits, orders, borders, the plan reveals that all ideas coexist in interspatial dynamics and communication. This is the history of civilization (from an Anglo-Saxonish point of view, true), an overview of the world of thought and inventions as transferred into ink – this is how we live, how we think, in a semi-organized, floating sphere of intellectual dimensions.

There is an entrance but no exit, according to the map, and it's true. Die in here. That is the reality. Read on and argue, lighten up, get very lost, add what you can, understand and stick around.

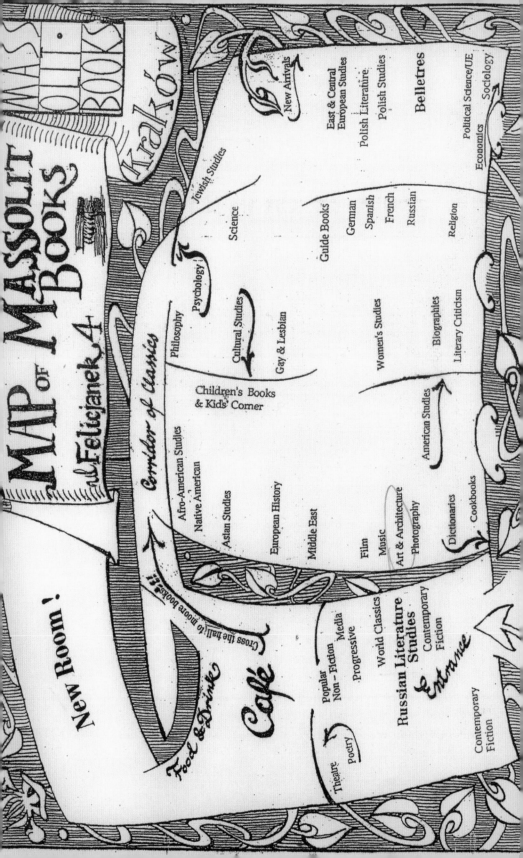

Sigurbjörg Þrastardóttir

Komisariat Policji I
KW-6151091R

Pólska lögreglan
spyr hvað pabbi minn heitir. Ég sé
ekki að hann hafi gert nokkuð af sér og
vil ekki nefna hann, því síður skírnarnafn mömmu
minnar eins og krafist er. Ég veit þeir munu fara
glæpsamlega rangt með nöfn þeirra. Ég
veit að í skýrslunni mun standa
að Thorstur og Gudmunga hafi hist og
kennt hvort annars, eins og í biblískri sögu, og úrslit
þess ekki orðið betur heppnuð en þögul kona með
röndótta húfu sem er ekki einu sinni fær um
að passa eigur sínar. Eins gott hún á ekki
barn sjálf, því hefði sennilega verið stolið
líka.

Pólska lögreglan býr ekki þröngt, en fátt er í raun
innanstokks. Ofnarnir eru á hjólum. Stólarnir við
skrifborðin eru ekki á hjólum.

Pólska lögreglan er skræfa. Þegar regnið eykst á
kvöldin eiga liðsmenn hennar allir óvænt erindi
á stöðina – draga þangað hverja
einustu bullu, ökuþór og lánlausan veg-
faranda, til að sleppa við að þramma eftirlitið í rigningunni.

Ég stend kviknakin
í máðum klefa
á gömlu og mjög köldu hóteli og yrki
um pólsku lögregluna. Þegar ókunnugir hafa
farið kraflandi höndum um eigur manns og þar
með sjálfan mann er nauðsynlegt að
vatnið renni.

Pólska lögreglan lætur mig
undirrita sannleikann.

Ég letra annan sannleika með
fingri á óstöðugan sturtuklefa, ég banka, ég
segi far ég segi angur segi vel og þeir kinka
kolli án þess að skilja
vel því túlkurinn er ekki kominn og ég stend
í lappirnar og ég verð
að vera vakandi í hávaðanum í rennandi
eldgömlu vatninu í sturtuklefanum því
ef hnífur er
til að mynda hafinn á loft hinum megin móðunnar
mun það ekki bjarga mér að tilkynna hvað
mamma mín og pabbi heita.

Sigurbjörg Þrastardóttir

Komisariat Policji I
KW-6151091R

The Polish police
inquire about my father's name. I can't
see he's done anything wrong so I won't give
it away, nor my mother's Christian name,
which is required next. I know their names will be
criminally misquoted. I know the report
will say that 'Thorstur' and 'Gudmunga' met and
knew each other, as in a Bible story, with the
sad result of a quiet woman in a colourful hat
who can't take care of her belongings. Just as well
she doesn't have a child of her own, or surely
that would have been stolen too.

The Polish police are not cramped but
the station has few furnishings. Radiators have
wheels. Chairs behind desks have
no wheels.

The Polish police are sissies. When the rain grows
heavy in the evenings, every officer has a sudden
errand at the station, dragging in every single
drunkard, driver and hapless passer-by,
so he doesn't have to march in the rain.

I'm standing completely naked
in a worn out cell
in a freezing old hotel writing
lyrics about the Polish police. When strangers have
shuffled your belongings and thereby shuffled
your self, the water must run.

The Polish police make me
sign the truth.

I draw a different truth with
a finger in an unsteady shower, I knock, I
say be I say longing I say well and they
nod without understanding very
well for the interpreter isn't here yet and I
stand on my
own two feet and I must
be alert in the noise from the running
ancient water in the shower for
if a knife for example
is flung high on the other side
of the fog it will not save me to say what
my mother and father are called.

trans: SP/ZS

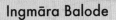

Ingmāra Balode

Īzāka un Esteres ielu stūris, Kažimeža, Krakova

kur čīgā kafejnīcās kur singera šujmašīnas bez neviena dzīpara
berzējas gar ienācēju pirkstiem tīksmīgi
nokrikšķ durvju kliņķis
nokrakšķ plecs

nočīkst parkets
atzīšanās čukstus iet pār dakti:
zini
es apēdu šokolādi
ko biji noslēpusi atvilktnē
un ko tu noteikti taupīji brokastīm
tā bija tik rūgta
un garda*

čīgā kafejnīcā un tu izbrīnījies saki paskaties kā snieg
aiz gandrīz uzzīmētas rūts
bet fonā šokolādes jēzu toms veits dūc

* šajā vietā pasmaida viljams karloss viljams.

Ingmāra Balode

On the corner of ul. Estery and ul. Izaaka, Kazimierz, Kraków

someone's scraping strings in the cafés where singer sewing machines
without a single thread
are soothed by customers' fingers
a handle creaks
a shoulder cracks

parquet squeaks
a confession goes whispering across
the candle's wick
you know
I did eat the chocolate
you had hidden in the drawer
and which you were probably saving for breakfast
it was so bitter
and delicious*

someone's scraping strings in the cafés
amazed you say look how it's snowing
beyond the drawn-on window pane
in the background the quiet buzz
of tom waits singing chocolate jesus

*at this point william carlos williams smiles

trans: IB/ZS

Zoë Skoulding

In Kazimierz, Kraków

for Ingmāra Balode

the green tea sachet on the saucer
is proof that I've been to the café in your poem
     where the tables are old sewing machines
waiting for chance encounters with umbrellas

outside
     the snow that fell in your poem
        has turned to drizzle
and seeped through the stitching of my boots

   a row of heads stretches out
        behind a candle
but none of them contains the poem
     sleeping in the cracked mirror

street names thread the city
     wicking up the past
  to flare in Esther Street where
in the marketplace I tried on someone else's clothes
   they didn't fit it doesn't matter but

so much depends
upon

a red-curtained
window

glazed with rain
water*
          violins
on the stereo
      scraped strings from
just around the corner in another time
where frozen music thaws on the tongue

*at this point William Carlos Williams sighs

Zoë Skoulding

Nowa Huta

proof I've been east to the steel town
　　that's part of someone else's story
　　　　is a crumpled ticket in my pocket
　　　　　　stamped on the number 4 tram

every compass point is marked
　　by a road every archway leads
　　　　to a courtyard a turned page a tilt
　　　　　　in the day's identical rhythm

I steel myself against the lines
　　of songs sleeping in the concrete
　　　　where windows hold their breath
　　　　　　pulled to the centre I sleep

in the machine of narrative
　　the Avenue of Roses blooms
　　　　beyond flakes of rust
　　　　　　rain from the ceiling

Sigurbjörg Þrastardóttir

Centrum B
(Nowa Huta)

LoL
(við getum ekki hlegið, bara skrifað það)

útópía
átta krákur
sólskríkt
glerhús

steingráir barnavagnar sjoppur
og kappleikir
í splunkunýju virki
hugmyndanna

Centrum B (er þá ekki lengur centrum, er það) ég bjó
þar og átti stutt pils, dúkku-
lísur úr hnauspappír

happy go lucky
við hverju býstu
býstu
?

að kvenlega strompa beri
við himin í
hamingjuátt, hárrétt

(já, við túlkum gleið bros á veggi)

ég klippti út:
stál
verk
smiðjurnar
ég klippti allt
út úr
hnausheiminum í
stutta pilsinu

Sigurbjörg Þrastardóttir

Centrum B
(Nowa Huta)

LoL
(we cannot laugh, only write it)

utopia
eight crows
sungiggling
glass houses

rock-grey prams kiosks
sport events
in that spunky new fortress
of ideas

Centrum B (then it isn't a centrum, is it) I lived
there, I had a short skirt, paper
dolls from thickpaper

happy go lucky
what do you expect
expect
؟

that feminine chimneys
rise against the sky
in the direction of happiness, how true

(yes, we translate wide smiles onto walls)
I cut out:
the steel
the works

I cut
everything out
from the thickworld in
my short skirt

trans: SP/ZS

Zoë Skoulding

it's a city that asks questions, gives no answers

for *Sigurbjörg Prastardóttir*

we may still cry in taxis
    though behind the window
it's not winter the electricity
    grids are humming
there has never been a word
    for crossfire in this language
shuffle the deck which one
    will you choose how will you
construct a house of cards
    so the stones won't fall
below the currency the city
    has thirteen hearts and none of them
is beating the circulation
    gone you play your hand
in this uncertain state
    it was not a heart attack
when he fell his ear
    pressed to the ground for
six-month-old information
    or digital toxic waste
grassed over the carbon cost
    of data cold enough to handle
she signs five times to say yes
    this is the whole truth all of it

*Note: the title and first line are adapted from 'H and H
(und Leipzig)' by Sigurbjörg Prastardóttir.*

Elżbieta Wójcik-Leese

Taking 'walk' for a walk

    a line going for a walk (Paul Klee)
    ganga means to walk and a walk, which is feminine
                                   (Sigurbjörg)

520d WYPOCZYWAĆ (verb: TO REST)
         leisure
               leisurely walk in Polish
spacerować
pospacerować
przespacerować się
            prefixes elon-
                 gate the
space

         gate inch open : pobłąkać się (wander)   błąkać się
    błąkać   błąkam   łąka (meadow)

            pochodzić
    przechadzać się   to and fro up and down (the meadow?)

           połazić (ramble)
                przejechać się so no meadow
                    instead a track-and-town

przejechać się spacerem (go for a ride at leisure)

go   therefore   TO GO (czasownik: CHODZIĆ)
          in Polish also: court
                  visit
                  tend
                  circulate

wear
function
revolve
roam

Rome? not
in Greek: HODÓS
via/way

DROGA/ROAD   to walk

spacerem
space   to   roam

a word on its walk

Zoë Skoulding

Walking –

Old Norse: valka to drag about
Old English: wealcan to roll

Wheat fibres stretch kneaded to bread
under the hand's drag and roll

as fulled cloth thickens under
the foot scouring wool matted

to a waulking song where
generations have trod, have trod,

as tread turns to trade and walks
all over you. What these boots are

made for: here they come on air/water.

Walking –
The body is tilted forward from the basic standing
position and the weight thrown on the ball of the foot,
while the other thigh is lifted and the leg and opposite
arm are swung forward (fig. 6B). Various muscles, aided . *

The ball of the foot rolls over
sprung tendons into a stride

(strive, a fight gathered into the limbs) –

the pull of sinews kneaded
and released – rolling air,

rolling the ground into itself.

*at this point William Carlos Williams walks out

Sanna Karlström

50 ways to walk in Finnish

To walk: kävellä, astella, astua, askeltaa, kulkea, kuljeskella, käydä, patikoida, jaloitella, tepastella, tallustaa, saapastella

To walk (slowly): tallustaa, talsia, laahustaa, laahautua, kömpiä, lyllertää, löntystää, lumpustaa, luntustaa, lampsia, lompsia, rämpiä, tarpoa, raahustaa

To walk (fast): kipittää, kipaista, ravata, painella, viuhtoa, harppoa, kiirehtiä, koikkelehtia, viipottaa, marssia, panna tossua toisen eteen

To walk (with short steps) :sipsuttaa, köpittää, köpöttää, töpöttää, piipertää, käppäillä, tepastella, tepsuttaa, taapertaa

To walk (silently): hiipiä, hipsiä, hiippailla, tassutella

Julia Fiedorczuk

Droga. Wyjście

My, zarażeni, musimy stale ponawiać wezwanie.
Inaczej znikniemy.
Wchłonie nas ciemna noc jeży i mrówek.
Przerośniemy pleśnią.
I wsiąkniemy w grunt.

My, zarażeni, musimy stale ponawiać wezwanie.
Wpuszczać w siebie to zabójcze morze.
Bo trudno uwierzyć w pustkę, której nikt nie widzi.
Trudno nie szukać. Choćby po omacku.
Kimkolwiek jesteś podaj mi swój głos.

Kimkolwiek jesteś podaj mi swoje ciało języka
i dnia. Proszę, wyciągnij dłonie.
Dotknę cię lekko jak czas.

Kimkolwiek jesteś podaj mi swoje ciało nocy.
Zliżę sól z twoich chłodnych powiek.

I zobaczysz świat.

My, zarażeni, musimy wszystko zaczynać od nowa.
Więc pozwól, że ukocham twój mrok.
Co w tobie rośnie, niech we mnie zakwita.
A owoce tych kwiatów niech ciebie nasycą.

Kimkolwiek jesteś biorę cię ze sobą.
Chodźmy.
Inaczej znikniemy.
Popatrz, tu jest droga.

A tu nie ma mapy.

Julia Fiedorczuk

Road. Exit

We the infected are bound to renew our summons.
Or else we'll vanish.
We'll be absorbed by the dark night of hedgehogs and ants.
We'll sprout mould.
The ground will soak us up.

We the infected are bound to renew our summons.
To let the murderous sea enter us.
It's hard to believe in emptiness that can't be seen.
Hard not to seek. To grope at least.
Whoever you are, pass me your voice.

Whoever you are, pass me your body of language
and day. Please, extend your hands.
I shall touch you gently as time.

Whoever you are, pass me your body of night.
I shall lick salt off your cold eyelids.

Then you will see the world.

We the infected are bound to keep starting from scratch.
So let me love your dark.
May what grows in you blossom in me.
May the fruit of this bloom satiate you.

Whoever you are, I'm taking you along.
Let's go.
Or else we'll vanish.
Look, here's the road.

And here's no map.

trans: EW-L

Ingmāra Balode

ģeometrija

es vēl biju ceļā, bet pavēlā plauksta jau lauza vārgākus oleandrus
un citas radības dārzā aiz žoga, kur botāniski nepieskatītas nātres
dzelzīm smaržoja pāri.

es vēl biju ceļā, bet to meiteni, kas nupat izkāpa no melna auto,
ome jau gaidīja mājās vai māte – iznākusi nama priekšā, augšā
viens gaišs logs, nekāda prieka, zilā halāta kabatā lakats,
otrā – atslēgas, jaušams pēc tā, kā pievelk roku.

es vēl biju ceļā, bet kāds taipus dārza vārtiem sauca draugu, kāds
skaitīja Tallinā zvaigznes,
kāds Grācā pagriezās uz otriem sāniem, kamēr es prātoju, kā
labāk tulkot viņa
dzejoli „czworobok" – drīzāk četrskaldnis, nevis četrstūris, tikai ne
kubs.

ietinkšķas zvaniņš uz stūres.
es vēl ceļā, bet Zolitūde guļ, ā, nē, kaimiņš staigā ar suni.

nepieraduši sasveicināties, tomēr uzsmaida kādam,
kas, skaitīdams augusta kartē punktus,
pieradinās pie ceļa.

Ingmāra Balode

geometry

I was still on the road, but dusk's fingers picked out brittle
oleanders and other creatures down there in the botanical garden
behind the fence, untended nettles sending up their scent.

I was still on the road, but a mother or grandmother shuffled
on the doorstep for that young girl who'd just stepped out
of the black car – a bright window above her, no pleasure,
a scarf in one pocket of her overall, keys in the other, I could
see by the way she moved her hand.

I was still on the road, but on the other side someone was
yelling a friend's name, someone was counting stars above Tallin,
someone turned on his side in Graz
while I was on the road wondering how to translate
his poem 'czworobok' – maybe a tetragon, maybe a square,
but not a cube.

A bell tings on a handlebar.
I'm still on the road, but Zolitūde is sleeping, or, no, look,
there's a neighbour walking a dog;

we don't usually say hello, but still he does spare a smile
for me, joining the dots on the map of late August,
getting used to the road.

trans: IB/ZS

Ingmāra Balode

uz lidostu

tu it kā brauc uz lidostu man pakaļ
bet patiesībā sēdies taksī un brauc tikai atpakaļ
dūmi šoferim pīpējot sitas pret stiklu kā akvārijā
balss netrāpa telefonā trāpa tajā parkinga kartē
it kā uz lidostu
bet atpakaļ (amerika pārvēršas salā) savelkas dūrē
(gaisa atsvaidzinātājs cauri prērijai šūpojas fūrē)
pirksti ar ogli kāds zīmē to putnu no dzejoļa g. a. spirti nožūst
(arumi saritinās)
un izlīst tuša tev klēpī
neviens nekad nedzied par vīrieša klēpi
vēl vairāk bail vēl vairāk noslēpums
bet tādas domas var izdomāt gaisā

kilometri
vertikāli
starp mums

Ingmāra Balode

to the airport

it seems you're on your way to the airport to pick me up
but you're just getting in the taxi to go back,
the driver's smoking, smoke pushes against aquarium glass,
a voice misses the phone entirely and enters the parking meter
instead

to the airport – it seems –
but in fact you go back (america shrinks to an island) crumpling
into a fist
(in the car, air freshener sways through a prairie)
fingers and charcoal, somebody drawing a bird from a poem,
apollinaire's alcools drying out
(ploughed fields folded up)
ink flows on to your lap
why does no-one ever talk about a man's lap
even more terrible even more – a secret
see what thoughts can appear in the air

kilometres
vertically
in between us

trans: IB/ZS

COLOUR WALKS

COLOUR WALKS
COLOUR WALKS
COLOUR WALKS
COLOUR WALKS
COLOUR WALKS

Ana Pepelnik

so many colours

A note about colours
is colourless.
Just black and white.

Black letters
resting
on white paper.

But I've walked
the green park
for you collecting

the colourful world
for your
tiny fist.

Zoë Skoulding

Bangor Mountain

someone's flung aside
    a pair of jeans
        plastic
lids of bottles
    cardboard
  from an instant barbecue

and only the sky picks anything up

glazed roof of the arcade (empty now)
  forget-me-nots under our feet

this sky you speak across
      your voice
bouncing off rock

     the city
flashes back
  a blue drone of traffic

as if in the distance all that's disparate
    could be caught
in the echo of one voice
    a single colour

Overleaf: Sanna Karlström: *A white walk*

55

Sigurbjörg Þrastardóttir

silvia í heimsókn

'þessir eru undarlegir tímar',
segir silvia

himinninn hefur misst
tak og tvístrast yfir landið innanvert

sést fleygur á stórum flutningabíl
sem skutlar rúðum
á litlum sítróen sem lagt er á skakk
í bergstaðastræti
sést og blýnegldur flekkur
á gömlu bárujárnshúsi undir holti

flísarnar úr himni vorum
eru víða
í auga barns á mýrargötu
í verkfæraskála sem horfir yfir olíusund
í leðurjakka í mínu eigin aftursæti
flygsa kemur meira að segja
til mín á ullardragt frá sjöunda áratugnum
þetta vítt
hefur himinninn tvístrast

og það tekur því ekki að hósta, silvia

því ljósskærblá sárbrynnandi tármúsabrot
úr himninum yfir okkur öllum
eins og við vorum

munu fylgja þér heim

Sigurbjörg Þrastardóttir

silvia visiting

these are strange times,
says silvia

the sky has lost
its grip and shattered across the land, inward

see a slice on a huge van
delivering windows
on a small citroën parked sideways in
bergstaðastræti
see a double-nailed patch
on an old ironbound house on the slope

the splinters from our sky
are elsewhere, too
in the eye of a child in mýrargata
on a tool hut overlooking an oil slick
on a leather jacket in my own back seat
a flake even comes to
me on a woman's wool suit from the sixties
that's how wide
the sky has scattered

and you can save the coughing, silvia

for lightbrightblue sorequenching teardragging fragments
from the sky over
who we were

shall follow you home

trans: SÞ/ZS

Julia Fiedorczuk

Pola Mokotowskie

Co mi po tych chmurach? Deszczu
po coś mi? Po co mi bezdomność
skoro ty nie jesteś

drzewem? Teraz nie do ciebie,
deszczu. Chciałabym się schować
w domu twoich liści.

Kiedy coś zapiszę, to nie muszę
Czytać, uwierz: gdybym mogła
byłabym krzakiem bzu

pod którym odpoczywasz
w ten bezchmurny dzień.
Twój deszcz mnie obezwładnia.

Julia Fiedorczuk

April in Pola Mokotowskie

What's the point of these clouds? Rain,
what good are you? What on earth
is the point of being homeless
if you are not

a tree? No, rain,
not you. I'd like to shelter
in the house of your leaves.

When I scribble this down, I don't have to
read it, believe me: if it were possible
I'd be a lilac tree

under which you'd rest
on a cloudless day.
Your rain overcomes me.

trans: JF/ZS

Julia Fiedorczuk

Deszcz

Wiosno, twoje soki
płyną po palcach drzew.
Wiosno, twoje włosy
na których się kładę
żeby być stworzeniem!
Kto powiedział
ludzkie? Kto
cokolwiek mówi?

Coś mnie dzisiaj kocha,
to pewne! Burzo,
czy wiesz co znaczysz?
Twój grad białych kwiatów
dedykujesz komu?
W twoim czarnym domu
pocałunki mnożą się
jak motyle. Twoje ramiona,

wiosno, gdy spadam.
Litości,
Uwierają mnie
twoje łodygi!

Julia Fiedorczuk

Rain

Spring, your saps
flow down the fingers of trees.
Spring, your hair,
where I lie down
to be a creature!
Who said
'human'? Who
says anything?

Something loves me today,
for sure! Storm,
do you know your own meaning?
Your torrent of white blossom
– who is it dedicated to?
In your black house
kisses breed
like butterflies. Your arms,

spring, when I fall.
Mercy,
your stalks
prickle me!

trans: EW-L

Elżbieta Wójcik-Leese

Untranslated Words on Another Tongue

Do they inscribe difference unfamiliarity doubt a guessing game risk taking chance adventurousness colonizing zeal archival timidity global aspiration pride?

Cognitive shortcuts, entry points

Detours

Do untranslated words sketch a route through a 'foreign,' written in a different language, text which could be retraced? By whom?

Weaving untranslated words into a text composed in another tongue is wandering through a foreign city where a perceivable grid (the concept of the city, its map) underlies unfamiliar names. It deploys them.

Can such a stroll through the text hint at the identity of the original walker/writer? How does the other reader, in another tongue, experience this dislocation? Or is it a location?

How can Latvian, Slovenian, Polish, Finnish and Icelandic be found through underneath in-between English words? Rendered into recognizable signs of map-charting: gaps, blanks, shortcuts, detours ...

Triangulating

Reading English as an 'interlanguage.' Not the ultimate language of translation.

The bridge language, yes, but what about the two banks it spans? The whereabouts of the banks and the bridge on the city's map?

The logic of this movement?

On the tip of my tongue.

Which?

Sigurbjörg Þrastardóttir

beitt
eða *steliþjófur*

ef ég myndi einhvern
tíma þekja tabula
föla
á hinu málinu
yrði það um
höfuðstaðinn minn
því mér þykir vænt um hann
það yrði um
rangt um
eitthvað rétt um
heita sívalninga
í heitum lófum
það yrði glæpur
allra glæpa
á truflaða
hrámálinu
það yrði
misnotkun á
chmury
liście
bez handan við
svarta
upplýsinga
þrautina
það yrði sifjaspell
harmljóð á
röngunni yrði
ruddalegur
sleikur
koss
höggvið af
mér höfuð
á staðnum

chop
aka thief

if I'd ever
cover the tabula
white
in that other tongue
it'd be about
my capital
'cause i like it
it would be
about wrong about
something right
sweaty palms
wrapped around
warm cylinders
it would be
the crime of
all crimes
in that other cracked
tongue
exploiting
chmury
liście
bez just off
the black
malformation
highway
it would be
incest
the flip side of elegy
it would be
a deeply
brutal kiss
my capital
punishment

Zoë Skoulding

Variants on a Polish fragment

after Julia Fiedorczuk

this is glass this is *szkła* or *szkło* depending on where
it catches the light and I can't see anything through it
only hear the rasp of broken bottles
swept across a beach where I'm walking
towards you with bare feet in this variant
salt air wears the edges smooth

words are sharp against the town's low roar
but blur your ears and traffic turns tidal every step
leaves a white wave of salt on my shoes
in *wody wielkie* in vast waters I could
drown in the undertow of any language
in this variant it would make no difference

if green's as green as *zieleń* I am walking through it
scent of cut grass on the rubbish tip
overhang of leaves dripping on the pavement
in this variant I'm spit and shadow ticking inches
over earth's impossible face this is how close I am
when shades of meaning grow luminous

in this variant I'm split in glass with one face to the street
and one tilted into planes where colours
fold back in silence the smell of rain
vanishes in the future there is no drizzle only
specks of scattered shine across a lens
in this variant you can't hear me coming

Ana Pepelnik

thirteen days for the blackbird

the river is moving.
the blackbird must be flying.
Wallace Stevens

I.

winter was still
so very still
that we forgot
the beauty of inflections
when the blackbird sings
when it rains
and it just keeps singing

II.

the rain and the blackbird are one
but the blackbird lasts longer
as part of what i know

III.

the tram has outgrown the street
though it was the sun which
was shining so brightly
that you couldn't see the blackbird
even blacker under the rainbow

IV.

i don't know
who
saved the morning

that cherry tree
with open buds
or a song
about the blackbird

in the bright park
both
part of the evening

V.

i went through several cities
across squares into bright alleys
in every shadow the blackbird was resting

VI.

i'm looking into the nest
you're weaving
assiduously
singing three melodies

and it's april
dance dance black
bird and sing
about the beauty of innuendoes

VII.

circles
you discover only
when the blackbird flies
far to the edge
of one of many

VIII.

here...want a crumb?
one for a beautiful day
one for later
one for not stopping
for you.

IX.

it had to be in movement of wings
beneath the shadow cast on the ground
pierced only with clover
that had stopped growing

or in the wind's game caught in a bottle

X.

a tree doesn't fall
when three hundred blackbirds
fall asleep on it

when one single blackbird whistles
and accidentally sits
on a bonsai
centuries collapse

XI.

for seven days the sky was grey

a scrap of blue nearby
was a glare on grey sky
and only a blackbird flew low

XII.

on the edge of the moon you flew
because of may or the rain
today it's full
of silent overflights

XIII.

these days the river calmly
meanders

running under red and white
chestnuts

blossoms are lightly
dropping

between fingers turning towards
the clouds

but it's all in this
movement

like the rain that catches in the feathers
of a blackbird

trans: AP/ZS

Julia Fiedorczuk

Warszawa. 6:48

noc rozstępuje się cierpienie
wylewa się ze mnie
jak wino
na dnie tego naczynia
jeden opalizujący kamyk
w miejscu gdzie wszystko
łączy się ze mną i tą stertą
liści córeczko
którą wczoraj o zmierzchu
grabił pan w fioletowej
kurtce

Warsaw. 6:48

night parts suffering
pours out of me
like wine
at the bottom of this vessel
one opalescent pebble
where everything connects
with me and with this heap
of leaves, my little daughter,
that was raked yesterday
at dusk by a man in a purple
jacket

Warszawa. 7:03

otwieram oczy i te trudne sny
pękają
pod naporem światła
na dachach samochodów
ciepły błękit
boso
do kuchni
otworzyć okno miasto fala
uderzeniowa którą powstrzymuję
wznosząc ręce
do nieba

Warsaw. 7:03

I open my eyes and these difficult dreams
burst
under the pressure of light
on car roofs
the warm sky blue
barefoot
into the kitchen
to open the window the city the shock
wave which I hold back
raising my hands
to heaven

Warszawa. 10:23

moja kobieta jest okorowana
skłonna przyjmować ostre pocałunki
dnia który osiada na jej miękkich plecach
deszcz kryształ lód rozczochrana
mgła na czarnym trawniku pościel
z której szybko
znika osad snu

moja kobieta jest pęknięta wzdłuż płci
rozkochana w pustce która jest
która jest nią
kiedy stoi w oknie
jak w ramie obrazu
i widzi trawnik rozczochraną mgłę
obok czerwonych samochodów

Warsaw. 10:23

my woman is bark-stripped
keen on receiving sharp kisses
of the day that settles on her soft back
rain crystal ice unkempt
fog on the black lawn the sheets
quickly shed
their sediment of sleep

my woman is cracked along her sex
head over heels in emptiness that is
that is her
when she stands in the window
as in a picture frame
and sees the lawn the unkempt fog
beside the red cars

trans: EW-L

Sanna Karlström

Whirlpool

minä katselin televisiosta ulos siellä mekaaninen mamma pesi lattiaa
autot kuin hitaat kiiltävät kovakuoriaiset ylittivät siltaa ja lentokone lensi vapaana
ja hyväksyin sen että koneet pyörittävät pyykkiä ja puhdasta sähköä
joka syttyy tästä napista vähän kello kuuden jälkeen eikä pimeässä enää muuta tähdellistä

minä katselin televisiosta mitä sieltä tuli valon nopeudella koko Amerikka
koskelin ruutua joka erotti minut naisesta joka oli palannut koneistettuun keittiöön
ja valmisti jotakin mustavalkoisesta kohinasta kammatuille lapsille

aviomiestä ei näkynyt, ehkä hän sotilasasennossaan odotti tilaisuutta astua valaistuun
teräksiset ruokailuvälineet liukuivat laatikostossa edestakaisin
valon kulma lepatti tuuli käynnisti sateen nosti sitä kohti

76

Sanna Karlström

Whirlpool

Through the television I was watching a mechanical mother washing the floor
cars like slow shining beetles were crossing the bridge and a plane was flying free
and I accepted the machines churning laundry and the pure electricity
that flares up from this button just after six and there is nothing significant in the dark any more

Through the television I was watching what arrived with the speed of light the whole of America
touched the screen that divided me from a woman who'd gone back to the mechanical kitchen
to make something for children scraped up from black-and-white

couldn't see the husband, maybe he was standing in his military pose waiting for his moment
to step into the shining steel cutlery was sliding about in the drawer
lights on the corner fluttered wind started the rain lifted towards it

trans: SK/ZS

Sanna Karlström

Aikoinaan puhuttiin paljon siitä
että monumenttia tulisi siirtää lähemmäs ministeriötä,
jotta patsashenkilö osattaisiin yhdistää siihen.
Toisaalta patsas olisi silloin
vaikuttanut rakennusta mahtavammalta.
Ministeriö antoi luvan siirtää taivasta kaksi metriä taaksepäin.

Previously there were many discussions
as to whether the monument should be relocated nearer the ministry
so people could associate the statue with it.
On the other hand the statue would then have appeared more
magnificent than the building.
The ministry gave permission to move the sky two metres back.

trans: SK/ZS

Ingmāra Balode / Julia Fiedorczuk / Ana Pepelnik / Zoë Skoulding / Sigurbjörg Þrastardóttir

Ljubljana Walk

Let me wrap you around me my dear golden city.
Hooded by your northern suburbs I'll slip out of sight
and land near the river, so quiet today.
Fish like broken flashlights under the water
thrive on the blood of our farthest dreams
separating river from stream,
feet from the bank, the walk from our feet.

Sigurbjörg Þrastardóttir

Handmade Cities

A bridge in Ljubljana has just been renamed Japanese Bridge by a local girl, because groups of Japanese tourists tend to stop there to take photographs. Another street is Meeting Street, because that's where she by default has appointments with her friends. On the same map, a local poet has marked the place where he always has coffee and renamed the street Coffee Road.

I'm thinking how I would rename the streets of my city, were I entitled to. Roughly, I'm thinking Aragata instead of Skólavörðustígur, because my friend Ari runs a photograph shop at the bottom of it. I'd put Flugbraut (Runway) instead of the new Hringbraut, for it has five lanes and looks like an airport, and I'd dub Hafnarstræti as Morðport (Murder Alley). And so on.

We distributed copies of Ljubljana maps to local people, the guests of our poetry walk and others, and those maps had had the original street names removed. A colleague of mine back in Reykjavik helped erasing the names. Another colleague, a graffiti artist, inscribed on it: Handmade City – Ljubljana. The guy at CopyLand in Ljubljana helped operate the copy machine, then I did the rest myself. When I was paying, he asked how many copies I'd made. I said ten. When asked if he wanted to verify that, he replied: No, I believe you. I don't have time but to believe you.

This is how people help each other, trust each other, and collaborate in making things, projects, visions. Entire cities, even. This is how Ljubljana has been made through its centuries; through plans, accidents, favour exchange, conversation, hard work, madness and destruction. It has resulted in the city we see today, and the names we see on today's tourist maps. But it could have been quite a different city, with different names, if different people had been in charge. Or if we had checked in at a different time in history.

With our handmade map of Ljubljana we invite people to (re)name their city as if they were in charge – to slide their everyday life into the official aspect of the city, to share memories, to shape the Ljubljana aura, to personalize their home-city which in its own right is a very personal entity to the inhabitants. We encourage them to translate experience and habits into words and names, to wear the private everyday on the formal outside – in short, to turn everything inside out.

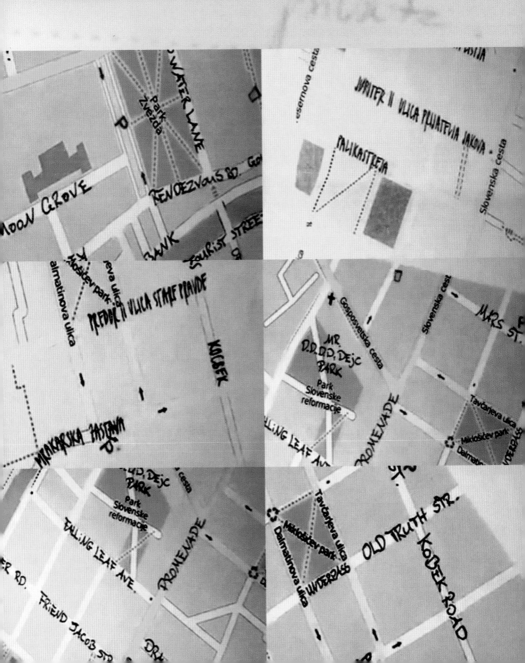

Ingmāra Balode / Julia Fiedorczuk / Ana Pepelnik / Zoë Skoulding /
Sigurbjörg Þrastardóttir

Rhythm: A conversation with Ljubljana

Wcześnie: ściany oddają mnie światu i jestem
widzialna – niewidzialna – widzialna
na szorstkim chodniku
z którego wycieka noc –
rytmiczna naprzemienność słońca i cienia –

visible – invisible – visible
at the red light sudden noise
of feet and words takes me over and
through buildings in a rhythm of light –
dark – lighting up the unnamed street

poglej noge v nogavicah ljudi. prihajajo
iz kluba in končajo na postaji. gledajo
v različne smeri. okoli njih stojijo znaki
prihodov in odhodov. v temi se mesto zguba.

Skellur á svelli hvellurinn þegar fellur ís
úr höndum unglings.
Smellirnir í vélinni sem gerir meira,
alltaf meira.
Hellirigningin sem skellur taktföst –
taktlaus – taktviss, alveg endalaus, á stéttinni þar sem ísinn
seytlar.

Hér gildir að hlaupa hratt
gegnum hjarta borgarinnar
ógnarhratt
eins og hjartsláttur
áður en regnið nær þér
áður en kellingin rukkar.

Áður en kellingin rukkar, aftur, í tvígang
taktlaus – taktvís – handalaus.

Oddycham, oddycham, oddycham, zamykam oczy
i słyszę śpiew życia, słyszę, jak mnie wyśpiewuje
wielogłosowo, wielorytmicznie, polimetrycznie,
to jest moje serce
pulsujący szary kwiat
wielogłosowo, wielorytmicznie, polimetrycznie,
od stóp po końce włosów

a grey pulsating flower
Ljubljana crosses morning
the streets beginning to sun
I cross the square in
strides heartbeats strides
skin crossed by shadows again the leaves turn
bells say time say resonance
I am a note in the city's polyphony
between the seconds breath evaporates
and everyone is speaking
at the same time

pilsēta pazūd. bet vietā nāk soļu ritms,
vietā nāk kraukļu švīkas nomales smiltīs,
ilgsti šajā pilsētā, ilgsti, ar tevi tā vienā smilkstā
izbirst starp riteņiem, izšķīst starp mākoņiem,
saplīst sīkās sarkans-zaļš-sarkans dzirkstelēs.
līs pār tevi kā lietus, mirks viņas krāsās pirksti.

po kantah za smeti lije dež.
ko je mimo se nadaljuje v lužah
ta vdih ko se odprejo dežniki
ta izdih ko se zaprejo vrata pošte.
vsa ta muzika za nebotičnikom.

Sumt er ekki leyft á almanna-
færi, sumt sem færir sundur
læri, í skæri,
sumt sem særir
kenndir blygðunar

mublurnar slást í veggina
og leggirnir
teygjast og sveigjast og ljósakrónur
hrynja

fram og niður, upp og aftur
eins og stjörnur yfir torg
eins og glimmer yfir framstæða
maga í borginni

að ganga með vaknandi líf er í lagi
í gliðnandi rytma á almannafæri

að vekja lífið
hraustlega, hratt
er hins vegar
alveg
bannað í borginni
úti – en inni – eru reglurnar – úti
úti – inni – úti – inni

outside – inside – outside – inside
I am faces on billboards on the other
side of someone's skin that doesn't burn
in the sun of early September
rhythm of loose change in my pocket
adding up the columns step after step
through glass as windows run through me
becoming glass against stone and wood
the day fragments in voices stuttering on surfaces
breaking into pixels

thud of bass under my sleep over and over
in the grip of the city's rhythm
sleeping in the broken wires

the window teaches me
the rhythms of another language
as rain hammers on the tiles my tongue
hits the roof of my mouth
wait
I'm listening

Julia Fiedorczuk

Urban bodies

In *Rhythmanalysis: Space, Time and Everyday Life* Henri Lefebvre suggests that in our observation of the world we should move beyond things and images in order to become sensitive to the various rhythms which constitute the sensible reality. 'Everywhere where there is interaction between a place, a time and an expenditure of energy, there is rhythm', he says.[1] Lefebvre's 'rhythmanalysis' is a radical exercise in that it constitutes a critique of what he calls 'the thing' and 'thingification' (reification) characteristic of late modernity with its cult of commodities and images. The rhythmanalyst does not stop at the appearance or (fetishistic) market-value of objects but delves into the 'scandal of the sensible': '[h]e thinks with his body, not in the abstract, but in lived temporality.'[2] 'He' – for Lefebvre consistently uses the masculine pronoun to refer to the human subject – comes close to the poet. That is because poetry, too, defies 'thingification' through its sensitivity to rhythms, to the sensuous rather than strictly rational aspects of thought, to the bodily rather than exclusively symbolic dimensions of language.

One might therefore suggest that the genuinely poetic experience of a city relies on a sensitivity to its various rhythms. What are those rhythms? They have to do with repetitions and cycles of human and non-human pursuits and processes. They are generated, on the one hand, by diverse social activities, such as work and entertainment and, on the other hand, by natural cycles such as the alternation of the seasons, of day and night, the life processes of the body which, too, consists of 'a bundle of rhythms, different but in tune.'[3] Of course it is not possible to distinguish sharply between the natural and the social, as these are merely concepts. Much has been written lately on the loss of nature due to the fact that the natural environment has been affected by technology pretty much everywhere on the planet. But it is perhaps worth pointing out that, while techne modifies nature, it also grows out of what is naturally given (it requires the natural resources, it utilizes the laws of physics, etc). Therefore, the cyclical life of nature is not only the background for our social, linear times, but also, quite literally, their grounding. This 'interpenetration' (John Cage's term) of the natural and the social is an important aspect of urban life too. Though traditionally identified with civilization and opposed to the more 'natural' settings such as the farm or wilderness, cities, too, grow out of the earth. No matter how far-reaching the urban transformation of nature may be, cities still have to breathe, eat and drink. They take pleasure in the green of their parks and in the past many cities used to be built on rivers (Kraków, Ljubljana, Warsaw, the cities we visited with Metropoetica, are all structured around rivers). It is the intersections and the overlaying of the human and the non-human, of what is produced by civilization and what is not anthropogenically generated, that interest me in my work as a poet. The embodied human subject whose experiences and crises I am attempting to express inhabits precisely this ambiguous space: a space whose limits are marked, one one side, by animate and inanimate matter and, on the other side, by meaning. In what way do specific cities pose – or impose – meaning on physical and biological reality? How can this meaning be read, mis-read and/or challenged?

When walking in a city one adds one's own rhythms to the already existing polyphony. It is a physical exercise – one's muscles are employed as well as one's sight, hearing and intellect. Walking without a pragmatic purpose – I am going to call it 'radical walking' – makes one open to what Virginia Woolf described as the 'shocks' of perception. Those shocks momentarily penetrate what the same author labeled as 'the cottonwool' of our normal non-existence. And it is in those 'shocks' – in things making themselves present to the embodied subject, in the merging of the inner and the outer (rhythms) – that poetry originates. Radical walking we have been doing as part of the Metropoetica project served, to my mind, the purpose of stimulating such 'shocks' in order to allow the participants (not only the poets but also, for instance, the audience we took with us on our poetry walk in Ljubljana) to shake off the automatism of our normal perception of space, which tends to be especially strong if it is a familiar setting. Experimental walking of the sort we have been practising is defamiliarisation, to use the term coined by Victor Shklovsky. It allows for a renewed experience of urban space, for the production of new meanings and for reaching beyond meaning, for the poets as well as – hopefully – for the readers of their poems. Metropoetica has been, to me, an exercise in (re)reading, which has employed both the rational (symbolic) and the sensuous (material) aspects of my being.

Henry David Thoreau in his celebrated essay 'Walking' associated his own practice of radical walking – he referred to it as 'sauntering' – with spiritual freedom, claiming that 'in wildness is the preservation of the world'. Walking without purpose (at least four hours a day) was for Thoreau a necessary condition of physical and spiritual health. Speaking, a bit condescendingly, of mechanics and other folks working indoors, as well as women who were confined to the house', he wondered half-jokingly how it was possible that these people had not yet committed suicide. Even though the environment of Thoreau's excursions was 'nature' as opposed to 'civilization', the outdoors as opposed to enclosure, he chose to use the word 'wildness' rather than 'wilderness' to characterize the spaces he traversed. Now wildness, I wish to propose, implies not only a type of physical setting but also a certain spiritual quality. Understood in this sense must wildness necessarily be opposed to the city? Walt Whitman, Thoreau's contemporary and his spiritual kin, celebrated cities – 'populous' cities – in several of his poems. A hundred years after Thoreau and Whitman, in 1950's and 1960's, at least two American cities – New York and San Francisco – became the scenes of a revolt that has since been described, more than once, as 'pastoral.' The main actors and the followers of the Beat Movement, which spelled out a powerful questioning of the meaning of America, readily accepted the non-conformist ideals of their 19th century protoecological predecessors, yet the centers of their rebellion were urban.

The term 'urban pastoral' has been coined in recent years to describe certain types of city poetry (including Whitman's urban poems). Fundamental to any discussion of urban pastoralism is a conviction that it is in the city, or perhaps in some specific cities, at specific historical moments, that one can find the spaces of semiotic play characteristic of the pastoral. The semiotic play, or the ambiguity of the pastoral has to do with the fact that the central preoccupation of this kind of poetry is the situation of the human speaker in relation to nature and culture. In an insightful discussion of this aspect of pastoral poetry Greg Garrard proposes the term 'be/longing' (simultaneously longing and belonging) to describe the predicament of the human subject as represented by this type of writing. Humans both 'belong' in nature and 'long' for it (because, at least to some extent, they have lost it). This ambiguity, connected with the elimination of rigid identity categories, is where Garrard locates the possibly radical impact of pastoral poetry.[4]

Urban pastoral explores the semiotic possibilities offered by the city. City poets are, to use Timothy G. Gray's formulation, 'semiotic shepherds'. Gray discusses two American poets in this context: Gary Snyder and Frank O'Hara. Each of them was at some point at the center of a cultural movement that was in its essence pastoral. What is crucial, Gray notices that in each case it was the poet's body, his physical presence and mobility that was essential to the structure of the pastoral situation.[5]

All of the authors – poets, walkers, philosophers – that I have mentioned so far happen to be men. Traditionally it has been men who have had the required leisure to become engaged in idle walking and it has been men who have held the symbolic authority of the makers of meaning which, in turn, enabled them to map and re-map space. From Poe's 'The Man of the Crowd' through Baudelaire and Benjamin's *flâneur* to Frank O'Hara's, great city walkers have invariably been male. To walk the city in the body of a woman forces one to engage with a predominantly masculine tradition. Sometimes it means having to be confronted with the masculine gaze which has repeatedly reduced the woman to a passive object, a thing, an appearance. While it would be impossible and unproductive to reject the existing tradition of urban poetry in one's own attempts to read and write the city, I think the *flâneuse* has to mark her difference from it. Metropoetica has been to me a feminine project in that its central idea has been that the woman is a participant, observer and reader of the city life. In other words, she is the semiotic shepherdess, the maker of meaningful spaces, and not an element of the landscape. Her body is active, receptive, alive, it takes pleasure in what it feels and thinks, in being part of the human and inhuman commotion, an active body among other bodies. The *flâneuse* that I sometimes like to be also happens to be a mother of a little girl, therefore, when she walks, she must sometimes adjust her trajectory to that of her daughter. The little girl respects no straight lines, no landmarks, she is never in a rush. A pigeon or an ant can be as important as Warsaw's Palace of Culture or Saint Mary's Church in Kraków's central square. The urban shepherdess stays alert to all these small encounters and she would like to make her language welcoming and hospitable to various manifestations of being, to a rich polyphony of urban rhythms.

[1] Henri Lefebvre, *Rhythmanalysis: Space, Time and Everyday Life* (London, New York: Continuum Books) 15.
[2] Ibid., 21.
[3] Ibid., 20.
[4] Greg Garrard, *Radical Pastoral?* (The Green Studies Reader. From Romanticism to Ecocriticism. ed. Lawrence Coupe. New York and London: Routledge, 2000)
[5] Timothy G. Gray, *Semiotic Shepherds: Gary Snyder, Frank O'Hara, and the Embodiment of an Urban Pastoral* (Contemporary Literature, Vol. 39, No. 4, Winter 1998, pp. 523-559).

Ingmāra Balode

Rīga

Tas, par ko vislaik runājam, izpaužas kā bļodiņa pastas ar tomātiem,
ko meita, ietītu follijā, ved no tēva caur pilsētu mātei.
Norijuši savu klusēšanu,
sazinās tagad pār mūriem.

Tas, par ko mēs reiz mēdzām runāt,
iznirst riteņu starpā kā zālaina tumsa.
Vienreiz es braucu cauri pilsētai naktī,
ieraudzīju tevi stāvam vārtu rūmē un, kā atklājās,
lasām grāmatu. Somā siers un tomāti, un mēs
devāmies ieņemt svešu dzīvokli, kurā, kā atklājās,
jau kādu laiku dzīvoja mana māte,
atstājusi pie ledusskapja zīmīti,
aizbraukusi uz laukiem ravēt.

90

Ingmāra Balode

Riga

What we talk about all the time appears as a bowl of tomato pasta
wrapped up in foil, carried through the city by a daughter
from her father to her mother.
Both have swallowed their silence and now
send dishes and signs across the town.

What we used to talk about once
falls like shadows on grass between the wheels.
Once I rode through the town at night,
and saw you standing in the doorway by your bike and, it seemed,
reading a book. Olives and cheese in the bag, we set off
to occupy a flat in which, as it appeared,
my mother lived. Now
she'd posted a note on the fridge:
I'm off to the fields to do some weeding.

trans: IB/ZS

Zoë Skoulding

Windows

from behind closed windows
repeated in sleeping eyelids

from where I'm standing
late sun fractures glass

never so plainly meant
the waiting and watching

a flicker of lashes
in rapid eye movement

the city repeated I
repeat eyes and footsteps

rise to the surface
a history of daylight

or nervous system swarm
where trams hum softly

passing through glass splintere
foreign bodies under skin

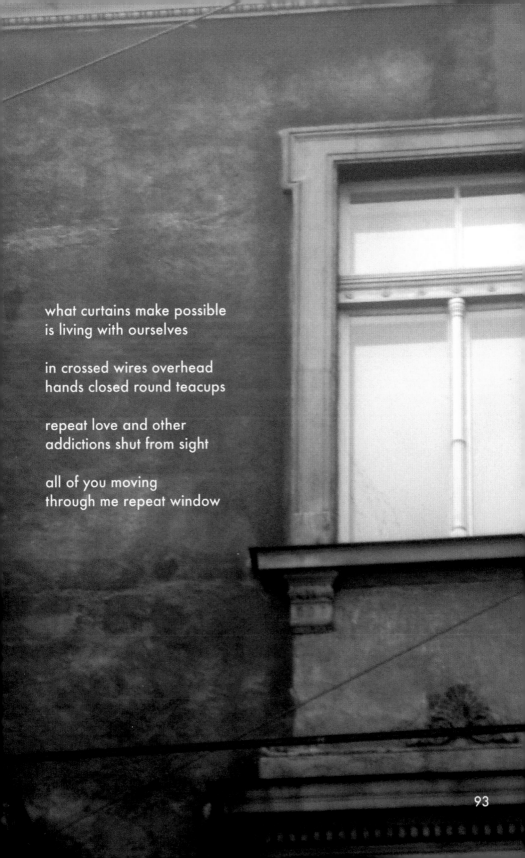

what curtains make possible
is living with ourselves

in crossed wires overhead
hands closed round teacups

repeat love and other
addictions shut from sight

all of you moving
through me repeat window

Elżbieta Wójcik-Leese

Logs:
A Record of Undressed Windows in Riga

i.

The offshore gust claims our small top window, *vindue*,
As it thrusts the balcony door against the bricks of 1936:
The golden age of Copenhagen masonry.

I text the exact measurements – the inner frame –
To our handyman already on his way to Poland.
Nine mirrors for a ballet school should soon be joined
By one glass sheet: 17.7 x 48.8.

ii.

one *okno*
one glass-eye
missing

iii.

eye-hole

iv.

those windows waiting for their
     glass

pain
     their proper panes
     not some flimsy dish-thin style
     but the double glazing that resists

the freezing fear of
gaping black

v.

enter a gap

enter a gap
enter a window
to keep a logbook of *logi*
the *logs* log

vi.

rubble up the hollow in hope

fill in the   hole
     the holes
     whole storeys of holes

     sedimentary absences

vii.

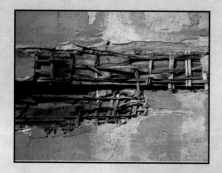

eye-sore

viii.

or the eye soaring to

> a quiet inlet in
> Riga's boisterous skyline
> moored by trolley-bus ropes

ix.

the windows of the sky then

openings in the firmament

or is it windows' heaven
where the drops of firm blue
linger on timber cross-beams?

x.

how to collect the blue drops
of sky, the lagoon
of cellophane
not transparent enough
to let the blue drop

xi.

lock the *log*

xii.

board the *ikkuna* up
so the icon of wind and eye
transcends its frame of reference

xiii.

carve the blue out of
rectangles and
squares
to seduce the gaze
back to the *gluggi*

xiv.

where the pane may
be redressed

where the corrugated blue
may refract the black
and capture the offshore
gusts in its sleeves of glass

xv.

in the sleeves of a blouse – wind

is that how I saw it?

xvi.

Gribi redzēt Rigu?

SADZĪVES
ATKRITUMIEM

JŪSU KONTEINERI APKALPO:

EKO RĪGA

0 8800
1 7600

WWW.EKORIGA.LV

Julia Fiedorczuk / Sanna Karlström / Zoë Skoulding /
Elżbieta Wójcik-Leese

Poem for Wrocław

The fountain pen runs its warmth along the length of Beethoven Street.

Limping though the passage, he aches with a teacup's brittleness.

A passing ship has dreamed her, smoking under the bridge.

He observes many possibilities of touch under the towel in the
hairdressers.

Here's a white bowl of tears: lie down.

The baby on the cushion is showing startling signs of growth, and so
is its hammer.

Walk carefully around the lamp; lick the depths of a Śliwki wrapper.

Courage: ignore the police, keep moving into blueness, whiteness

A branch of sleep unfurls down the staircase, counting each step.

The book's intention falls open in a basement.

The park is dying slowly in childhood photographs.

Why is she screaming in a shop, this woman who is unreachable in her anger?

Solace in gloves slips through June Rose Alley.

Nothing's in order, not even the invoices that she has carefully ironed.

What jumps out of the family photo is the shopping centre's mourning.

The idea of lost keys blows through the carpark.

Doubt shadows a pencil turning the corner.

A view of trams unfolds beyond the shaking birches.

Wind turbines caught in a single glance, a longing for cables and precision.

Transparency cuts through the alley, a sliced box behind glass.

Julia Fiedorczuk / Katerina Iliopoulou / Sanna Karlström / Zoë Skoulding

Utopia?

Where is the good place that does not exist?
Where does this unexpected joy come from?
And why does it settle on old stones, like sunlight?
What does it mean?
Who will you give the fragments of this modest paradise: rough skin on
the melon, an ice cube in a glass, the smell of sun on a child's cheeks?
Where will we put this moment for safekeeping?

Does a stone hold up?
If not, what's holding us?
When a person sits on a rock, how long does it take?
Is this stone original? If, how original can it be?

Why are there only eight personifications of wind on the top of this tower?
Why is there no winged figure for the breeze of tear gas and orange
blossom sweeping past the corner of the Polytechnic?
When was this and where is the original? Is beauty always dangerous?
Where is the missing head?
How long does it take to reconstruct a perfect human being?

If every step is a word, who will read the text you wrote by walking?
What do you swallow with eyes blinded by sunlight?
What do you let enter through your nostrils?
Can you choose between smells?
How do you make a monument from the dust of your shoes?

Why does history keep repeating itself?
When there is a war, is the country still beautiful?
Why is this day giving itself to me so willingly?
How much are the bananas? Your smile, is it priceless?
Who are all these questions addressed to?
Will the answer be made of words?
Do letters hold on to each other?
Could you hold me?
What is broken?

Are you made of paper? Or stone?
Why can't statues show their emotions in a public space?
Where's he going with the broken window frames and crumpled paper
he's extracted from the skip and piled up in his shopping trolley?
How far away do I have to be to look you in the eye?
Is it true that words on stone weigh more than words on paper?
Can you trust without believing? Where is the missing hand?
Can you believe without trusting?

What did you say to the woman who'd stood on that corner for forty
years? How many more hidden statues are there on the streets?
Why didn't you buy the lottery ticket?

Will you wait for me under this wise tree?
Will you wait for me?
Will the silence be understood as my inability to hear?
Will the silence be?
Will you wait for me?
Are you looking at me through the aeroplane window?
Are you getting smaller, or is it just me?
Can you show me where you are now?
When you fold the map, is the city closed?

Which is heavier, a cardboard house or a stone temple?
Where is the missing body? How do you keep a god in one place?
Why do banks look like temples?
What has been added and what has been taken away?
How do you keep a person in one place? How much does it weigh, this
wilting rose that you've been trying to sell me in a dozen different cities?

How do you ride the vertigo of the printed words on the walls?
What is there left?
And after the ride are you full or empty?
How do you find the word to begin again?
How do you find the place for one more step?

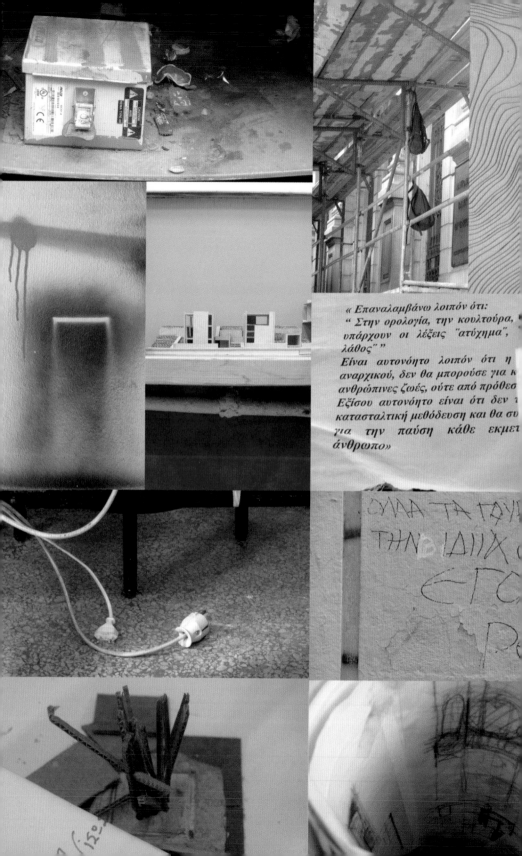

« Επαναλαμβάνω λοιπόν ότι:
" Στην ορολογία, την κουλτούρα,
υπάρχουν οι λέξεις "ατύχημα",
λάθος" "
Είναι αυτονόητο λοιπόν ότι η
αναρχικού, δεν θα μπορούσε για κ
ανθρώπινες ζωές, ούτε από πρόθεσ
Εξίσου αυτονόητο είναι ότι δεν 1
κατασταλτική μεθόδευση και θα συ
για την παύση κάθε εκμετ
άνθρωπο»

Elżbieta Wójcik-Leese

The Kinship of Six Languages: Translating as Writing

'Languages are not strangers to one another,' argues Walter Benjamin (in Harry Zorn's rendition into English), 'but are, a priori and apart from all historical relationships, interrelated in what they want to express.' Benjamin's notion of 'the kinship of languages,' pondered in his introduction to the translation of Baudelaire's *Tableaux Parisiens*, allows us to look beyond the typical translational trajectory: the movement from the source to a (temporary) destination.[1]

Two languages, two texts – the number two, foregrounded because prototypical, privileged because advocated by purists believing translation should proceed from a language thoroughly known to a mother tongue – can become three, when the third, mediating, language enters the relationship. Its appearance renders the translator's hesitations palpable. Bridging the linguistic and semantic gap, paradoxically it also gives shape to incomprehension and unfamiliarity.

What happens to the known and the unfamiliar when, instead of two or three, six languages search for their interrelationship? In 'The Task of the Translator' Benjamin claims that the kinship of languages reveals itself more fully and visibly in translations rather than in 'a vague alikeness between adaptation and original'.[2] The recommended plurality of intentions, which complement one another to hint at meaning, is literally more plural with the six languages of Metropoetica: Finnish, Icelandic, Latvian, Polish, Slovenian and English. To complicate this already complex interrelationship, the Metropoetica originals have been frequently composed in the second/foreign tongue, English, though their authors are not bilingual. Moreover, in this poetic project 'the translator' multiplies into translators who double as poets, subverting further the view of translation as a derivative use of language. Which language is derived from where? Which rhythms reverberate in which text? Is this text the source text or rather an intertext that insists on its in-betweenness? If 'in-betweeness' implies the number two again, should we rather talk about 'amongness'?

'Among,' as a preposition, derives from the phrase that meant 'mingling, assemblage, crowd.' Its *Oxford English Dictionary* definition first highlights 'the local relation of a thing (or things) to several surrounding objects with which it is grouped: Surrounded by locally.' The entry elaborates: 'In company, association, communion, or residence with or beside.' We might say, then, that 'among' denotes a space where a crowd is allowed, where things are assembled and where mingling can happen. Are six languages a crowd? Certainly they allow creative mingling as original texts are assembled. Is the space delineated by 'among' akin to the space of the city, which Metropoetica has sought to flâne? The rhythms of the city, the rhythms of the steps, the rhythms of the multilingual words and the rhythms of the thoughts maturing in them…

'For in its afterlife – which could not be called that if it were not a transformation and a renewal of something living – the original undergoes a change. Even words with fixed meaning can undergo a maturing process,' observes Benjamin.3 And the fixed meanings: of the city, walk, translation, translator, writer, creativity need to be revisited to stir them up, to begin their maturation.

In 1953 in Paris Paul Valéry publishes an essay on 'Variations sur Les Bucoliques' (*Traduction en vers des Bucoliques de Virgile*). In 1985 Denise Folliot publishes its English translation 'Variations on the *Eclogues*.'4 In 2006 Clive Scott quotes from the English version to demonstrate the affinity between translating and drafting, which – to this advocate of translation as (creative) writing – germinates a text perceived as unfinished, therefore potent in its multiplicity of meanings: 'The work of translation, done with regard for a certain approximation of form, causes us in some way to try walking in the tracks left by the author; and not to fashion one text upon another but from the latter to work back to the virtual moment of its formation…'.5

Valéry's 'walking in the tracks left by the author' transforms in Metropoetica into walking with the author, or even walking as the author. The now of translation and the then of writing collapse; the temporal distance to be traced back branches out into the present and the future. The space thus opened embraces not only the kinship of six languages, but also the kinship of writing and translating.

1 Walter Benjamin, 'The Task of the Translator: An Introduction to the Translation of Baudelaire's Tableaux Parisiens,' in *Illuminations*, ed. Hannah Arendt, trans. Harry Zorn (London: Pimlico, 1968) pp. 70-82.

2 Ibid., p. 74.

3 Ibid., pp. 73-74.

4 Paul Valéry (1953) 'Variations sur Les Bucoliques', trans. Denise Folliot. Reprinted as 'Variations on the Eclogues' in: *Theories of Translation: An Anthology of Essays from Dryden to Derrida*, ed. Rainer Schulte and John Biguenet (Chicago: U of Chicago Press, 1992) pp.113-126.

5 Clive Scott, 'Translating the Literary: Genetic Criticism, Text Theory and Poetry,' in: *The Translator as Writer*, ed. Susan Bassnett and Peter Bush (London: Continuum, 2006) pp.106-118.

Zoë Skoulding

Translating Cities: Walking and Poetry

While translation is often described as a secondary activity to literary creation, it is also associated with areas of knowledge and competence that suggest a different power relationship. The overview of urban space offered by the map may be compared with the professional expertise of the translator, who is traditionally expected to offer a transparent insight into another language and culture. The poet's navigations of language, meanwhile, in 'original' work or creative co-translation, may depend on chance connections and encounters in a performance of language that is more akin to the experience of walking through the city without a map. These contrasts lie at the heart of Metropoetica's activities.

To explore these ideas, one might turn to nomadism of the kind envisioned by Pierre Joris, who writes: 'A nomad poetics will cross languages, not just translate, but write in any or all of them.'[1] Writing across languages changes conceptions of space, particularly as it is experienced through the rhizomatic structures of online communication and contemporary possibilities opened by travel and globalization. The nomadic is a way of thinking about space that is also temporal: borders are crossed and re-crossed; categories do not stay still. The writer's knowledge is nomadic, and is less a question of defining categories than a practice of moving in and out of them. The city is a lived and inhabited structure that shapes and is shaped by its inhabitants, and the work of the poet is also part of different structures, which may be in tension with each other. It responds to local, national or international literary traditions, and to the production of culture within various local, national or international frameworks. Yet we may also think of writing as a communal but equally unpredictable and aleatory process that is as disobedient to structures as it is shaped by them. Geographer Doreen Massey argues for a conception of place as 'a constellation of trajectories' that 'poses the question of our throwntogetherness'.[2] The idea of a nexus of nomadic crossings in which space is open to time, and therefore to change, suggests a vision of urban experience that accommodates both individual and collective movement.

Knowledge, for the literary translator, is usually accepted as being knowledge of a language and culture, and the knowledge of the translator is defended through a sense of professionalism. Yet poets do not write as representatives of languages but as the makers of their own language: writing a poem might be compared with Paul Klee's conception of 'taking a line for a walk'; poetry is a form of not knowing, of following unfolding possibilities within language as it is explored. Translation creates further possibilities, each word and image presenting infinite choices to the translator.

Walking and the city

The city, rather than the nation, offers a social nexus of exchange that is more akin to the connections of virtual interaction; cities connect to other cities as much as to their surrounding areas. Yet they are places, too, and places in which women's ability to inhabit public space has historically been compromised. In the literature of the *flâneur*, epitomized by Baudelaire, the poet-observer of the city has been until recently almost invariably masculine. The feminine street walker, if she is noticed at all, has been characterized as a prostitute, someone who falls outside of legitimizing social structures. The poet in the city moves simultaneously through space and language. Poetic language, as Jean-Jacques Lecercle has argued, is disobedient to structure, formed by the constitutive remainder of sound and accident, and defined by a crossing of linguistic frontiers. Such frontiers are, in his view (drawn from the work of Judith Milner), 'linked to the speaker's experience of his own body', defined against what it is not.[3] He goes on to suggest:

> This is also how man experiences his body as a sexual body, as the body of a man and not of a woman, or vice versa. Perhaps this relation between the experience of language and that of the ascription of sexual roles is at the bottom of the parallelism . . . between the remainder in language and the Freudian unconscious . . . This is why frontiers are at the same time so entrenched and so compulsively breached.[4]

He describes language in both spatial and architectural terms, yet emphasizes the complexity and malleability of linguistic structures, which are 'not the imposing architecture of the Greek orders, but rather the crumbling castles of Victor Hugo's gothic sketches'. Nomadic frontiers in his view are not confined to poetic language but a condition of all language use, and one that can provide opportunities for writers since: 'a creative author can modify a frontier. She is not only an explorer, venturing into orderless and unruly territory, but also a ruler, who may decide to annex, temporarily or permanently, a small portion of the remainder'.[5]

124

As a means of exploring parallel lines between gender, writing, and walking in the city, I will outline some trajectories pursued within the collaboration of Metropoetica, conscious that each participant brought a different perspective to it, and that my own is necessarily partial. Poems were translated between Icelandic, Finnish, Slovenian, Polish and Latvian, whereas I am only discussing the interface with English. While all of the participants are women, the term 'women poets', it should not need to be said, is multiple and mobile, inviting a whole spectrum of responses. The category of 'women' as critiqued by Denise Riley is a linguistic frontier inhabited from diverse positions and should be understood as shifting over time. Gender identity fluctuates; one moves in and out of awareness of gender as a category, so that 'to speak about the individual temporality of being a woman is really to speak about movements between the many temporalities of a designation', whether these emerge in awareness of the body or others' perceptions of it.[6] Riley offers an example drawn from urban space:

> You walk down a street wrapped in your own speculations; or you speed up, hell-bent on getting to the shops before they close: a car slows down, a shout comments on your expression, your movement; or there's a derisively hissed remark from the pavement. You have indeed been seen 'as a woman', and violently reminded . . . that you can be a spectacle when the last thing on your mind is your own embodiedness.[7]

Yet, as Riley explains, this is only one aspect of a complex and changing story. In walking through the city, one passes through many different social, linguistic, economic and spatial relationships in which one's position as 'a woman' or even 'a woman poet' might mean something different. It is precisely the instability of the category that makes it at all useful, or even possible. The knowledge, then, that is negotiated in Metropoetica concerns how the practice of writing and translating poetry might bring together movements within city space, gender and language.

The analogy between city and readable text is made in Michel de Certeau's description of the view looking down on New York from the World Trade Centre. It is a view that offers fictional knowledge, a misleading vision of the whole. He describes how this view

> transforms the bewitching world by which one was 'possessed' into a text that lies before one's eyes.

transforms the bewitching world by which one was 'possessed' into a text that lies before one's eyes. It allows one to read it, to be a solar Eye, looking down like a god. The exaltation of a scopic and Gnostic drive: the fiction of knowledge is related to this lust to be a viewpoint and nothing more.[8]

By contrast,

The ordinary practitioners of the city live 'down below,' below the thresholds at which visibility begins. They walk – an elementary form of this experience of the city; they are walkers, Wandersmänner, whose bodies follow the thicks and thins of an urban 'text' they write without being able to read it. These practitioners make use of spaces that cannot be seen; their knowledge of them is as blind as that of lovers in each other's arms.[9]

It would be misleading to read this simply as a theory/practice binary, since the whole point of the passage is that both kinds of knowledge, from above and below, are integrated; the blindness of the walkers is observable only by contrast with the view of the city from above.

A question explored through Metropoetica is that of how to connect theory and practice, to link up a theoretical understanding with a practice of writing and translation. Movement between overview and ground level is enacted in an understanding of both urban space and the cultural spaces in which poetry is created. By considering walking and writing as parallel forms of knowledge in the parallel practices of different poets, our project has asked how the forms of knowledge engendered in the processes of writing might be understood through walking. What follows is my own journey, a written walk, through its process and some of the work produced.

Walking as a process

The first action of Metropoetica, before the participants had met, was a virtual *dérive* collaboratively directed through online maps. By walking in this way, we create our own text within the city's text. People usually walk for a reason, whether to get to work or go shopping. By contrast, a dérive, as developed by the Parisian situationists in the 1950s, is a way of walking without practical function:

126

In a dérive one or more persons during a certain period drop their relations, their work and leisure activities, and all their other usual motives for movement and action, and let themselves be drawn bythe attractions of the terrain and the encounters they find there. Chance is a less important factor in this activity than one might think: from a dérive point of view cities have psychogeographical contours, with constant currents, fixed points and vortexes that strongly discourage entry into or exit from certain zones.10

While the situationist dérive was above all an embodied experience of the city, our approach to it began as a textual and virtual one. Six poets in six different cities exchanged directions in order for each to go for a walk in their own locale directed by someone who had never been there. This involved each poet choosing directions by going for a virtual walk on her computer screen, trying to imagine what the satellite photos did not reveal, trying to feel which way she would want to turn at each junction if she were on the ground, perhaps being drawn left or right by the names of streets. Meanwhile, we kept in touch via an online forum, collecting and comparing impressions in prose as well as poetry, making connections between the cities in which we lived.

A collage of the directions themselves (p. 8) becomes a walk through different cities, an imaginative journey as described by Walter Benjamin, in which street names make a 'linguistic cosmos'.11 Although the map appears to offer a bird's eye overview, a control of space, it also reveals opacities in the unfamiliarity of names and the points at which the map breaks down. Each poet following the directions wrote individually about her journey, recording impressions in poetry or prose. Ingmāra chose to write directly in English, which, since this is neither her first nor second language, makes the poem already a form of self-translation. Her poem 'Victory' reflects layers of representation in a walk that remains 'virtual' even when it becomes embodied experience (p. 15).

A virtual walk
becomes more virtual as I turn
backwards and see
snow
changing my screen into a nameless street
on someone's unsigned postcard,
a few grey men falling
under a concrete flag.

Her response to a walk through Riga is preoccupied with time, not only with the histories signified by the city's monuments, but also the time of the collaboration, since we were working in different places with only the synchronicity of the different walks to connect us. Time is imagined in the poem in spatial terms through a play on the word 'March' to suggest both the month of the work's deadline and the activity of walking. Mars's masculine and military connotations are also echoed in the monument, which is ironically undercut, particularly in the oxymoron of the 'concrete flag', and the contrast of static symbolism of the past with a more urgent and mobile present:

> I'm walking in the snow,
> rushing towards the word
> I must conquer
> in this battle with
> the calendar. March.

Sigurbjörg, writing in Icelandic similarly registers the interplay between physical presence and textual representation. This poem was accompanied by a photograph of her reflection in the window of a post office in Reykjavik (p. 10).

> I watch myself
> watching myself
> in the clear glass
> in the mist
> watching the reader
> who then opens
> the book
> of course not
> holds it with
> green fleece mittens and
> doesn't dare to open
> the city

In both cases there is a sense that unmediated experience of place is beyond reach: in Ingmāra's poem the use of English implicitly connects walking through a Latvian spring with the 'everywhere' of online communication, while Sigurbjörg's poem is already turned towards the reader, to whom Reykjavik remains opaque and closed. Both poets recognize the city as a text; both are engaged in reading it (as in De Certeau's view from above), while simultaneously exploring the 'blind' knowledge of the walker at street level. It is this that differentiates these twenty-first century *dérives* from situationist practice in which the *dérive* was a means of replacing art with a form of utopian lived experience that, by overcoming urban alienation, would be revolutionary. Already saturated with media and communication, these globalized cities are experienced as being already texts, open to further translation and interpretation.

One might alternatively consider the *dérive* in terms of textual rather than physical mobility, in the sense that Maurice Blanchot uses it,[12] a term that, as Venuti points out, encompasses both the quality of being derived, in being formed from previously existing materials, and the drift, or movement.[13] The aleatory process of the situationist drift through a city is therefore evoked in the context of writing and rewriting. The city is a text through which the writer moves, and the text thus generated becomes the environment of the translator's *dérive* and offers scope for further derivation.

Metropoetica's second *dérive* was carried out collectively during our first meeting in Kraków in March 2009. We used a pack of cards to generate directions at each junction, agreeing on particular cards to indicate left, right, straight on, up, or stop and write. Weather conditions (it was raining and snowing) limited the time we were able to spend writing outside, but what gradually emerged as the exercise was repeated was a sense of how this medieval city drew us back to its centre. It was almost impossible to get lost, such was the centrifugal pull of the Rynek Główny, ringed by streets and then the Planty, a wooded strip where the old defensive walls had been. Yet the clarity of its structure was interrupted by building sites and roadworks, dug-up streets and patches of rough ground that diverted our walking and tripped us up. Sanna's poem 'Kraków' (p. 24), written during this walking, registers these gaps and disappearances:

> The park walked away
> I made notes on it
> as if someone had been humming a familiar tune
> and broken off.
>
> They picked up a plank as if lifting a piece of the street.
> They were grey inside and out.
> It was raining, my heart had dissolved inside my coat.
> A woman selling trinkets had a thought, surrounded by
> shine.

The poem plays with a reversal of humans and their environment: while the park is personified, the people are merged into their surroundings, their internal greyness and the dissolved heart recalling the unnerving absences of a Magritte painting. Within the even-toned description, city and subject are mutually constructive, the boundaries between them broken down. The process of translation, too, blurred the distinction between writer and translator, since it was negotiated into English from the original Finnish through Sanna's explanations and my own attempts to smooth the gaps and stumbles in the literal translation. Some of them are deliberately left in, like the encompassing 'shine' at the end that in its noun form in English usually refers to the surface of an object rather than to more widespread luminosity.

However, there were further areas to be explored. In some views of translation, an ideal of transparency gives readers the sense that they own a poem in a language that they do not speak, and the translator's process of travelling through the poem is often invisible. We were looking for ways of articulating movements through our languages that would parallel our walks through the city, and that would resist the illusion of transparency that English, as a global language, too easily offered. This led to a consideration of translation itself as a space to be negotiated.

The space of translation: détournement

The relationship between walking and writing may also be understood in relation to *détournement*, a term developed by the situationists to mean diversion or subversion of an existing text. Elżbieta suggested the use of untranslated words to create movement between languages within a single text:

> Weaving untranslated words into a text composed in another tongue is like wandering through a foreign city. A recognisable concept (a city, its map) which underlies, deploys unfamiliar names.

> Could this manner of moving through the text express the identity of the original walker/writer? How does the other reader, in another tongue, experience this dislocation? Or is it a form of location?

> How can the Latvian, Slovenian, Polish, Finnish and Icelandic be found through/below/in-between English words? Rendered into recognisable signs of map-charting. Gaps, blanks, shortcuts, detours...

In her reflection on walking (p. 44), dictionary entries are detourned in the situationist sense that in the recombination of existing elements, new or previously concealed meanings are generated or revealed through recontextualisation.14 Sanna, responding to the same idea, produced '50 ways to walk in Finnish' (p. 47), which through its list-like, thesaurus-type arrangement of words, foregrounds the concrete qualities of the text in both visual and verbal aspects. The reader who is not a speaker of Finnish encounters the text as a sound poem, or a series of hesitant steps in rough terrain as words are recontextualized within the frame of another language.

This approach situates the movement between languages not between original and translation, but within a single text. Sherry Simon points out that the terms for translation in Latin (*vertere*) and, mediaeval French (*turner*) allude to a practice understood as 'turning':

> A 'version' is a text which has been 'turned toward' a new language, 'turned into' a new book. But turnings are not always innocent, as we see in the related terms of 'inversion,' 'perversion,' or 'conversion.' While conversion carries positive connotations of repentance and redemption, of turning toward a new and better path, perversion is a turning away from conventional functions.15

Elżbieta's and Sanna's approaches uncover the ways in which the text turns away from interlingual relationships as commonly understood in the practice of translation, which often depends on a clear distinction between source and target language and culture. Translation tends to be, as Simon suggests, a means of separating and regulating; she adds, however, that 'when languages mingle . . . translation is put to the test'.16 Her points are made specifically in relation to the bilingual city of Montreal, but they would be true of many cities, particularly in the context of globalization. 'Every act of translation,' Simon writes, 'is a statement about human relations, about the ways in which languages, cultures and individuals are the same or different,' offering an expanded view of translation as a means of discovering and articulating otherness and identity.17 Meaning therefore oscillates between the old and new contexts, each 'turning' or per-/di-/sub-version extending the range of movements within the text.

Another means of widening further the space of translation is homophonic translation, or traducson, that responds to the otherness of a foreign language. Ana's poem *Trinajst dni za kosa* ('Thirteen Days for the

Blackbird') (p. 68), is already a version, drawing on Wallace Stevens's 'Thirteen Ways of Looking at a Blackbird'. It already contains a migratory aspect as a poem in Slovenian, written in Kraków, that responds to an American poem. As well as making with Ana the translation of the poem quoted above, I used the third stanza as the basis for an interpretation through sound (p. 26). Such 'translation' depends to some extent on willed ignorance, on working blindly with sound that is unhooked from language's ordinary communicative functions. What knowledge is gained through the process of writing when it depends on a rejection of, or blindness to, semantic meaning? I am suggesting that in examining the migratory and fugitive aspects of language, it is possible to discover poetic engagements in which the strangeness of the other tongue is not reduced to the clarity of the mapped overview. It becomes a journey through the foreign text that intensifies rather than reduces foreignness, leaving multiple meanings open. I was interested in how the process of responding to sound created opacity in English, as a hegemonic language, as a counterbalance to our practical use of English as a 'bridge language', another spatial metaphor. It is that very practicality that contributes towards the continuing imbalance of power between languages outlined by Lawrence Venuti, who advocates 'minoritizing translation,' which will resist assimilation by 'signifying the linguistic and cultural differences of the text – within the major language.'[18] My discussion of the texts generated during the project is limited in what it reveals in terms of knowledge about the particular cities in which those texts were written. Rather, I am interested in how the dynamics of the writing process can enable exploration of relationships between languages and spaces that are inhabited plurally, if we consider the city as Massey's 'constellation of trajectories'.[19]

Language and the Feminine

Gender, too, may be seen as one pattern of trajectory among others. While certain kinds of under-representation led to the decision to involve only women writers in Metropoetica, the participants themselves bring different opinions and cultural backgrounds to the relationship between gender and poetry, so it would be a distortion to suggest that the project presents women's experience or even 'women's poetry' as something discrete and identifiable. A more productive line of enquiry is suggested by Joan Retallack, whose notion of the Feminine as an aspect of language characterized by multiplicity and resistance to monolithic structure suggests a less restrictive frame through which to view the work of women writers.

132

Retallack's argument is that 'the feminine is in language from the start', and it is necessary to pay attention to this presence, a field explored largely by male writers such as John Cage and James Joyce.[20] In Retallack's view, a truly feminist poetics emerges when women take on a mode of writing that in its form reflects the social construction of the feminine, characterized by multiplicity, subversion and web-like patterns of interconnectivity. She notes that 'ironically, it's been particularly courageous for women to work in the territory of the Feminine, insofar as it can be called distracted, interrupted, cluttered, out of control'.[21] But to do so opens the possibility of an engagement with more complex patterns of understanding:

> Our Western cultural image resembles a brain with a severed corpus callosum — each side functionally innocent of the other. Did an evil surgery occur while we were all asleep in one fairy tale or another? One side happily thinks everything is simple; the other side unhappily thinks everything is complex. In this chronic bifurcation a potentially collaborative 'we' is missing the fact that complex dynamics aren't monsters lurking in forests, threatening the simple pleasures of blue skies. They are the forest. They are the blue skies. They are our entire natural-cultural environment.[22]

Retallack's stress on environment as both natural and cultural offers a means of understanding language's relationship with space, in that both are to be understood as 'complex dynamics', as movements within time that cannot be grasped through static representation.

As a means of exploring complex dynamics in both textual and lived spaces, Julia Fiedorczuk suggested during our second meeting in Ljubljana that we should use Henri Lefebvre's *Rhythmanalysis* as a basis for collaboration.[23] Following his view of the city as comprising multiple rhythmical and arythmical patterns, she suggested that we might take the city's rhythms as a starting point, and secondly that we might look for similar rhythmical patterns across our languages as a means of linking our contributions. Another starting point was the similarity of Lefebvre's key terms in all our languages – their Greek origins connecting them. In writing the poem, we became both observers and participants in the city's rhythms, tracking the movements of light and sound while becoming aware of our own motion through the crowds of walkers and shoppers. In 'Rhythm: A conversation with Ljubljana' (p. 82), my response to Julia's opening uses an echo of her second line to shift attention from the movement of night and day to that of the traffic lights, interweaving different scales and integrating natural and man-made rhythms. The poem continues across different languages, with echoes repeating the pattern of the opening; for example, in Ingmāra's Latvian: 'sarkans-zaļš-sarkans' ['red-green-red'] and Sigurbjörg's Icelandic: 'úti – en inni – eru reglurnar – úti / úti – inni – úti – inni' ['outside – but inside – the rules – are outside / outside – inside – outside – inside']. Alongside the writing of the poem we also used film to capture sound and image for a performance in which visual, aural and verbal rhythms were combined. This allowed us to integrate public interactions between our texts and the city. For one scene in the film, for example, Julia wrote the word 'rhythm' in chalk across the street, and we filmed bicycles, feet and shadows of passers-by crossing it. We also filmed each other standing motionless at different points in the city while shoppers and traffic rushed past. By meshing the reading of the poem with recorded sounds of the city and looped vocals, which we added live, it was possible to foreground language as sound among the other noises of the city, so that the mixing of languages within the text could be listened to with different kinds of attention. In our initial performance, the texts were not translated. As with homophonic translation, this approach creates a means of accommodating the foreign text in its foreignness, rather than taming it through translation. The city is explored in its unreadability, as patterns of sound moving across languages, rather than presented as a whole that can be grasped from a single cultural perspective.

In opening the process of translation to a range of cross-language movements, a text can unsettle a whole variety of structural relationships. Simon has, for example, drawn attention to the gendered positioning of translators, noting that: 'Translators and women have historically been the weaker figures in their respective hierarchies: translators are handmaidens to authors, women inferior to men'.24 The mixing of languages in collaborative writing and translation can therefore be seen as a critique of power structures in which gender emerges as a significant element. She discusses the work of Nicole Brossard and Christine Brooke-Rose, both of whom combine languages within a single text:

> By placing translation within the borders of their books, [they] smudge the distinction between original and secondary forms of writing, troubling (but not yet toppling) the entire edifice of conceptual complicities which maintains the power of author over translator, creation over reproduction, male over female.

The shape of these fictions reproduces the dividedness of identity, the ongoing – and never complete – negotiations between the mother tongue and the other tongue. The space of translation widens, becoming a territory in which the imagination settles down, takes up its ordinary existence.[25]

In making such a claim for translation's ability to unsettle conceptual structure, Simon's comment also indicates a dynamic within writing and translation that offers possibilities for envisioning both gender and cities, opening them to movement and change. Writing into the blind alleys of an unknown language, or relinquishing one's own overview to allow for a collaborator's different perspective, produces knowledge that is situated but not static, and always provisional.

1 Pierre Joris, A Nomad Poetics: Essays (Middletown CT: Wesleyan University Press, 2003), p. 38.

2 Doreen Massey, For Space (London: Sage Publications, 2005), p. 151.

3 Jean-Jacques Lecercle, The Violence of Language (London: Routledge, 1990) p. 24.

4 Ibid., p. 24.

5 Ibid., p. 19.

6 Denise Riley, 'Am I that name?': Feminism and the Category of 'Women' in History (Minneapolis: University of Minnesota Press, 1988), p. 98.

7 Ibid., pp. 96-97.

8 Michel de Certeau, The Practice of Everyday Life, trans. by Steven Rendall (Berkeley and Los Angeles: University of California Press, 1984), p.92.

9 Ibid., p.93.

10 Guy Debord, http://library.nothingness.org/articles/all/all/display/314 [Date of access: 14 June 2010].

11 Walter Benjamin, The Arcades Project, trans. by Howard Eilan and Kevin McLaughlin. Cambridge (MA: Harvard University Press, 1999), p. 552.

12 Maurice Blanchot, 'Translating' (1971), trans. by Richard Sieburth, Sulfur 26 (1990), 82-86.

13 Lawrence Venuti, The Translator's Invisibility: A History of Translation (London: Routledge, 1995), p. 307.

14 Tom McDonough, *Guy Debord and the Situationist International: Texts and Documents* (Boston: MIT Press, 2004), p. 196.

15 Sherry Simon, *Translating Montreal: Episodes in the Life of a Divided City* (Montreal: McGill-Queen's University Press, 2006), p. 119.

16 Ibid., p. 9.

17 Ibid., p. 12.

18 Lawrence Venuti, *The Scandals of Translation: Towards an Ethics of Difference* (London: Routledge, 1998), p. 12.

19 Ibid. 2, p. 151.

20 Joan Retallack, *The Poethical Wager* (Berkeley: University of California Press, 2004), p. 140.

21 Ibid., p. 94.

22 Ibid., p. 91.

23 Henri Lefebvre, *Rhythmanalysis: Space, Time and Everyday Life* (London: Continuum, 2004).

24 Ibid. 15, p. 1.

25 Ibid., p. 166.

Acknowledgements

Literature Across Frontiers
    www.lit-across-frontiers.org
Biuro Literackie
    www.biuroliterackie.pl
Vilenica Festival
    www.vilenica.si
Massolit Bookshop & Café, Kraków
    www.massolit.com
Port Wrocław
    www.portliteracki.pl
Latvian Literature Centre / Latvijas Literatūras Centrs
    www.literature.lv/en
Centre for Slovenian Literature / Center za slovensko književnost
    www.ljudmila.org/litcenter
FILI - Finnish Literature Exchange
    www.finlit.fi/fili
Iceland Literature Fund / Bókmenntasjóður
    www.bok.is
Polish Book Institute
    www.bookinstitute.pl
Dasein International Literary Festival / Dasein Philosophy Café
    www.dasein.gr
Christos Chrissopoulos
Riga Poetry Days

Zoë Skoulding would like to thank the Arts and Humanities Research Council fellowship in women's poetry and the city at Bangor University, which funded her participation in this project. A version of her essay 'Translating Cities' was published in *The Writer in the Academy: Creative Interfrictions* edited by Richard Marggraf Turley (Cambridge: D.S. Brewer 2011).

INGMĀRA BALODE

Ingmāra Balode lives in Riga, Latvia. Her debut poetry collection, *Ledenes, ar kurām var sagriezt mēli* (Candies to cut the tongue) (2007) was awarded the Best Debut Prize in Latvian Literature. Her poetry has been translated into Polish, Slovak, Ukrainian, English, Czech and Lithuanian. She is a literary editor and translator at ¼ Satori, a literature and philosophy portal and publishers (www.satori.lv). She has translated extensively from Polish and English, as well as from Czech, Slovakian, and Russian. In 2010, she was awarded the Prize for Poetry Translation by the literary magazine *Latvju Teksti* (Latvian Writings) for her translation of selected poems by the Polish poet Adam Zagajewski.

JULIA FIEDORCZUK

Julia Fiedorczuk is a poet, fiction writer, translator and lecturer in American Literature at Warsaw University, Poland. She has published four volumes of poetry, the most recent of which is *Tlen* (Wrocław: Biuro Literackie, 2009), a collection of short stories and a novel (*Biała Ofelia*, 2011). Her first poetry collection (*Listopad nad Narwią*) received an award for the best first book of the year (2003). She is also a recipient of the Hubert Burda Preis (Vienna, 2005). Her poems have appeared in anthologies in Great Britain, USA, Slovenia and Sweden. Her translations include English and American poetry, prose and criticism.

SANNA KARLSTRÖM

Sanna Karlstrom was born in Kokkola, Finland and now lives in Helsinki. She studied creative writing in Topelius Academy in 1994-1995, and has also studied folklore and aesthetics in Jyväskylä and Helsinki Universities. She has published three collections of poetry with Otava, most recently *Harry Harlow'n rakkauselämät* which was awarded the 2009 Dancing Bear Poetry Prize; her work has been translated into English, Russian, Estonian, German and Swedish, and has been widely anthologized. She has won several awards, including the 2004 Helsingin Sanomat prize for her first book.

ANA PEPELNIK

Ana Pepelnik lives in Ljubljana. She works as a presenter for the independent radio station Radio Študent and takes part in music-poetry performances. Her poems have been published in the journals of Literatura and Dialogi. Her first book of poetry *Ena od variant kako ravnati s skrivnostjo* (One Way to Treat a Secret) was published by LUD Literatura in the Prišleki series; her second book, *Utrip oranžnih luči na semaforjih* came out in spring 2009. Her translations of poetry into Slovene include the following: Elizabeth Bishop, James M. Schuyler, Matthew Zapruder (American Linden; Šerpa 2008), Joshua Beckman, Noelle Kocot, Matthew Rohrer. She was one of the four poets to be published in the 2011 anthology *In Unfriendly Weather: Four Slovenian Poets*.

ZOË SKOULDING

Zoë Skoulding lives in Bangor, Wales. Her most recent collection of poems, *Remains of a Future City*, was published by Seren in 2008, following *The Mirror Trade* in 2004. Her collaborations include *Dark Wires*, with Ian Davidson (West House Books, 2007) and *From Here*, with visual artist Simonetta Moro (Dusie, 2008). From 2007 to 2012 she held an AHRC Fellowship in the Creative and Performing Arts at Bangor University, where she is now Senior Lecturer. She has been involved in several projects incorporating poetry, film and music, and is a member of the group Parking Non-Stop whose album *Species Corridor* was released by Klangbad in 2008. She is editor of the international quarterly Poetry Wales.

SIGURBJÖRG ÞRASTARDÓTTIR

Sigurbjorg Prastardottir is a writer and columnist in Reykjavik, Iceland. Her debut collection of poetry, *Blálogaland* (Land of Blue Flames) was published in spring 1999, followed the year after by a collection of road-poetry, *Hnattflug* (Circumnavigation), which was voted best poetry book of the season by staff-members of Icelandic bookstores. As well as poetry she has written dramatic and prose texts, and two novels: *Sólar saga* (The Story of Sól) – which won the Tómas Guðmundsson Literature Award when it was published in 2002 – and *Stekk* (Jump) in 2012. Her poetry has been translated into several languages and published in anthologies in Germany, Sweden, Italy USA and the Netherlands. A bilingual collection of her poems in Icelandic and English (translated by Bernard Scudder), *To bleed straight*, was published by Forlagið in 2008.

ELŻBIETA WÓJCIK-LEESE

Elżbieta Wójcik-Leese translates contemporary Polish poetry into English. Her translations appear regularly in journals and anthologies, such as *New European Poets* (2008), *Six Polish Poets* (2009) and *The Ecco Anthology of International Poetry* (2010). In 2011 her versions featured on the London Underground. *Salt Monody* is her selection from Marzanna Kielar (2006); *Nothing More* presents her translations of Krystyna Miłobędzka's poetry (2013). She co-edited *Carnivorous Boy Carnivorous Bird. Poetry from Poland* (2004). She co-edits peer-reviewed *Przekładaniec. A Journal of Literary Translation* (Kraków, Poland). As a Fulbright scholar, she examined Elizabeth Bishop's archives, which resulted in *Cognitive Poetic Readings in Elizabeth Bishop. Portrait of a Mind Thinking* (2010). She lives in Copenhagen.

KATERINA ILIOPOULOU

Katerina Iliopoulou is a poet, artist and translator who lives in Athens. Her poetry has been translated into many languages and has been featured in literary reviews and anthologies in Greece and abroad. She has participated in international writing and translation programs, festivals and Biennials. She has published three books of poetry. Her first poetry book (*Mister T.*) received the Diavazo award for best debut. As a member of the arts collective intothepill she has co-organized projects that bring together poetry and visual arts. She has translated poetry of Mina Loy, Robert Hass, Ted Hughes and Sylvia Plath. She is co-editor of the bilingual site greekpoetrynow.com

Photo credits:

Sanna Karlström - 11, 12, 13, 56, 57, 112, 113, 114, 115, 116, 117
Ana Pepelnik - 18, 19, 100, 101
Zoë Skoulding - 9, 34, 35, 39 (top), 45, 78, 79, 80, 81, 90, 91, 92, 93, 121 (part), 122 (part), 144
Sigurbjörg Þrastardóttir - 10
Elżbieta Wójcik-Leese - 94, 95, 96, 97, 98, 99
Karol Pęcherz - 104, 105, 106, 107, 108, 109
Alan Holmes - cover, 22, 23, 37, 39 (bottom), 43, 46, 47, 82, 83, 84, 85, 121 (part), 122 (part)
Christos Chrissopoulos - 121 (part)
Massolit Bookshop 29